DATE DUE

SEARCHING
FOR
RECOGNITION

Recent Titles in
Contributions to the Study of World Literature

SEARCHING FOR RECOGNITION

The Promotion of Latin American Literature in the United States

Irene Rostagno

Contributions to the Study of World Literature, Number 72

GREENWOOD PRESS
Westport, Connecticut • London

Library of Congress Cataloging-in-Publication Data

Rostagno, Irene.
    Searching for recognition : the promotion of Latin American
literature in the United States / Irene Rostagno.
       p.   cm. — (Contributions to the study of world literature,
ISSN 0738–9345 ; no. 72)
    Includes bibliographical references (p.   ) and index.
    ISBN 0–313–29869–6 (alk. paper)
    1. Latin American literature—20th century—Appreciation—United
States. 2. Latin American literature—20th century—Translations
into English—History and criticism. 3. Books and reading—United
States—History—20th century. 4. Frank, Waldo David, 1889–1967—
Influence. 5. Alfred A. Knopf, Inc.—Influence. 6. Center for
Inter-American Relations—Influence. 7. Corno emplumado.
I. Title. II. Series.
PQ7081.R7 1997
860.9′98′0904—dc20   96–22008

British Library Cataloguing in Publication Data is available.

Copyright © 1997 by Irene Rostagno

Library of Congress Catalog Card Number: 96–22008
ISBN: 0–313–29869–6
ISSN: 0738–9345

First published in 1997

Greenwood Press, 88 Post Road West, Westport, CT 06881
An imprint of Greenwood Publishing Group, Inc.

Printed in the United States of America

The paper used in this book complies with the
Permanent Paper Standard issued by the National
Information Standards Organization (Z39.48–1984).

10 9 8 7 6 5 4 3 2 1

Copyright Acknowledgments

The author and publisher gratefully acknowledge permission to reprint the following:

"Latin American Literature and the Alfred Knopf Collection" by Irene Rostagno. Originally published in *The Library Chronicle* 22 (1983): 17–49. Reprinted by permission.

"Waldo Frank's Crusade for Latin American Literature" by Irene Rostagno. Originally published in *The Americas* 46, no. 1 (July 1989): 41–69. Reprinted by permission.

Letters to and from the editors of *The Plumed Horn/El Corno Emplumado*. Reprinted by permission of the Harry Ransome Humanities Research Center, The University of Texas at Austin.

Selections from a 9 October 1963 letter from Thomas Merton to Margaret Randall reprinted by permission of the Merton Legacy Trust.

Selections from a 10 July 1976 letter from Gregory Rabassa to Ronald Christ reprinted by permission of Gregory Rabassa.

Selections from a 29 January 1968 letter from Alastair Reid to Edgar reprinted by permission of Alastair Reid.

Selections from letters dated n.d. 1966 and 26 October 1966 from Edward Dorn to Margaret Randall reprinted by permission of Edward Dorn.

Selections from a 10 December 1965 letter from Robert Kelly to Margaret Randall reprinted by permission of Robert Kelly.

Selections from a 23 July 1975 letter to Carmen Valcells, a 12 June 1975 letter to Carlos Fuentes, and a 2 September 1977 letter to Luis Harss reprinted by permission of Ronald Christ.

Selections from a 27 April 1964 letter from Lawrence Ferlinghetti to Margaret Randall reprinted by permission of Lawrence Ferlinghetti.

Selections from a 16 June 1964 letter from Blanche Knopf to John Brown reprinted by permission of the Knopf Archives, The University of Texas at Austin.

Selections from a 31 March 1966 letter from Cid Corman to Margaret Randall reprinted by permission of Cid Corman.

Contents

Acknowledgments

I am grateful to the many individuals at various institutions who helped me in the preparation of this manuscript. At the University of Texas at Austin, I owe very special thanks to Professor William Stott, whose encouragement, generosity, patience, and lucid editing inspired me to complete this manuscript. I am also grateful for the early support and guidance of my work by Professors William Goetzman (who originally suggested the topic), Naomi Lindstrom, and Robert Crunden. I also want to express my gratitude to Dr. Dave Oliphant for his invaluable comments and unflagging support throughout these years. His colleague Tom Zigal was also very helpful in the beginning.

Friends who gave their time and effort to help me with my research and writing are Elizabeth Horan, Abelardo Avendaño, and Amalia Pereira.

The resources of the Harry Ransom Humanities Research Center at The University of Texas at Austin, the Charles Patterson Van Pelt Library at the University of Pennsylvania, and the Center for Inter-American Relations in New York were indispensable to my research. I have quoted from the following collections with permission: Alfred A. Knopf Publishing Files and *El Corno Emplumado* Collection, Harry Ransom Humanities Research Center of the University of Texas at Austin; Waldo Frank Collection, Rare Book Collection, University of Pennsylvania; and the Literature Program Archives, Center for Inter-American Relations. I am also indebted to Ms. Cathy Henderson and Dr. Neda Westlake at the Harry Ransom Humanities Research Center and the University of Pennsylvania, respectively, for making available important material. To Ms. Rosario Santos and Ms. Lori Carlson of the Center for Inter-American Relations, as well as Mr. Daniel Shapiro of its successor, the Americas Society, I also express my thanks for all their help and understanding. Particular appreciation goes also to Mr. Russell Marks, who authorized me to go through the files of the Center for Inter-American Relations and to Mr. William A. Koshland for permission to quote from the Alfred A. Knopf Papers. I am also indebted to Ms. Barbara Spielman at The University of Texas Press for allowing me to work with publishing files on Borges, Paz, and Rulfo.

Chapters 1 and 2 of this book appeared, in somewhat different form, as articles in *The Americas* and *The Library Chronicle of the University of Texas at Austin*. Their respective editors, James Riley and Dave Oliphant, provided most valuable help and criticism.

Other important sources of information were critics, editors, publishers, writers, and translators with whom I corresponded or conducted interviews.

I owe a great debt of gratitude to Dr. Ronald Christ for his insightful comments, and permission to quote from them and letters he exchanged with Latin American writers. His ideas gave me a perspective I could not otherwise have gained. Particular thanks go to Mr. Lysander Kemp, who patiently answered my questions and made valuable suggestions, and Mr. James Laughlin for his extremely helpful letters. I quote with their permission. Acknowledgment is also gratefully made to Mr. Allen Ginsberg, Mrs. Waldo Frank, Ms. Sara Blackburn, Ms. Eleanor Antin, Mr. Ernesto Cardenal, Ms. Margaret Randall, Ms. Denise Levertov, Mr. Ed Dorn, Mr. Lawrence Ferlinghetti, and Mr. Robert Kelly for allowing me to quote from their letters in various collections. I wish also to record my indebtedness to the many people with whom I discussed issues raised in this study: Mr. Emir Rodríguez Monegal, Mr. Thomas Colchie, Mr. Alastair Reid, Mr. Gregory Rabassa, Mr. Arturo Fontaine, and Mrs. Gabriela Canfield, among others.

Last, and most important, my husband, David Madison, daughter, Annette, and parents, Victor and Lucy Rostagno, have provided constant material and spiritual support for this endeavor. I dedicate this book to them, for without their love and encouragement it would not have been written.

Introduction

Until quite recently inter-American cultural relations were largely a one-way street. Though for more than a century Latin Americans have read works of North American writers,[1] the reverse has not been true. Interest in writing coming out of Latin America was restricted to the narrow circles of college Spanish and Portuguese departments. Then came the 1960s and the "boom" in Latin American literature, which changed things dramatically. More Latin American novelists and poets than ever before were reviewed, translated and read in this country. In this study I describe how this change came about, focusing on those Americans—writers, critics, publishers, and editors—who in a fifty-year period struggled to make Latin American letters known to the U.S. public.

While the story to be told in the next four chapters is set in this century, the roots of inter-American intellectual and artistic exchange can be traced as far back as the late 1600s. At that time Cotton Mather "set himself"—as he said—to learn Spanish in order to disseminate Protestantism in the predominantly Catholic Hispanic colonies. Literary relationships between the United States and its southern neighbors thus began, appropriately, motivated by extra-literary concerns, polemics in fact.

In the early nineteenth century, Argentine essayist and educator Domingo Faustino Sarmiento happened to grow up reading Benjamin Franklin's *Autobiography*, which he later translated into Spanish in the hope that the new South American nations would emulate their northern neighbor's ingenuity and pragmatism. As he noted after having traveled extensively in Jacksonian America: "The United States is unique on earth. There are no unconquerable habits that retard for centuries the adoption of an obvious improvement. . . . There is a predisposition to try anything."[2] From his travels in the then barely settled Northwest Territories in the late 1840s, and from his reading of James Fenimore Cooper, he came to the conclusion that the literatures of the Americas shared common ground. Despite the fact that he failed to stir up interest for Cooper's lengthy novels in either Argentina or Chile, he managed to get his novel, *Facundo: Civilization and Barbarism*, published in this country in 1868. Translated by his friend Mary Tyler Peabody Mann, Horace Mann's wife, the book was the first major Latin American work to be translated and published in America. A generation before Sarmiento, in 1827, "Ode to Niagara" by Cuban poet José María Heredia had appeared in the *United States Literary Gazette and Review* in an English version by William Cullen Bryant; it left hardly a trace.

With the emergence of American expansionism in the 1880s and 1890s, cooperation of the sort Sarmiento advocated became impossible. Latin Americans felt distrust of, if not overt hostility toward, their big neighbor to the north. An important spokesman for this new attitude was Cuban poet and essayist José Martí, who lived in New York and worked as a correspondent for *La Nación* of Buenos Aires and other Latin newspapers between 1881 and 1895. Although he admired the energy and "marvelous prosperity" he saw around him, he deplored the plight of American immigrants and factory workers. As a vocal opponent of America's hemispheric policies, he became a defender of what he considered to be the "superior spiritual order" embodied in Latin American culture.[3] Despite his disapproval of American foreign policy and materialism, Martí wrote essays on American writers Walt Whitman, Mark Twain, and Ralph Waldo Emerson and translated American books—Helen Hunt Jackson's novel *Ramona*, for example. Martí's work stimulated interest in American literature throughout Latin America.

In the aftermath of the Spanish-American War, the essay *Ariel* (1900), by Uruguayan José Enrique Rodó, emphasized even more the distinctions Martí had made between the two cultures. Using Shakespeare's *The Tempest* as a metaphor, Rodó portrayed Latin America as Ariel—spiritual, idealistic, and religious and the United States as the crude, materialistic Caliban. Though simplistic, his essay spawned a myth that is still a compelling one for Latin American intellectuals. Where Sarmiento proclaimed that the two cultures had much in common, Rodó emphasized their deep differences. Through the first decades of the twentieth century, Rodó's central assumption informed nearly all Latin American writing about the United States.

Even mildly political writers, like Nicaraguan poet Ruben Darío, borrowed the essay's symbolism. In 1904 he denounced Teddy Roosevelt's invasion of northern Colombia, now Panama, in a poem that addressed the president and all Americans in these terms:

> You are the United States,
> future invader of our naive America
> with its Indian blood, an America
> that still prays to Christ and still speaks Spanish.[4]

While Latin American writers paid a great deal of attention to America in its period of greatest hemispheric imperialism, United States writers evinced substantially less curiosity about their neighbors to the south. Charles Dudley Warner's accounts of his Mexican travels, published in *Harper's* in the late 1880s, quickly fell into oblivion. Stephen Crane's Mexican tales and articles written in the mid-1890s were no more significant.

The Mexican Revolution of 1910 was the first event in Latin America to elicit widespread interest among American intellectuals. The uprising held great appeal for a young and politicized generation of writers. Dissatisfied with social conditions in America, they saw in Mexico's grass-roots movement possibilities for cultural renewal. The large number of authors who traveled south between 1910 and the late 1920s makes the Mexican Revolution the obvious starting point of a study concerned with the American preoccupation with Latin American writing in this century.

Choosing the figures on which to focus is more difficult. Jack London, John Reed, Anita Brenner, and Katherine Anne Porter are just a few of the many for whom Mexico, rather than Paris, was the foreign place in which to come of age. The list of those who passed through is no less impressive and includes Hart Crane, Lincoln Steffens, and the English writer D. H. Lawrence.

Of all American artists and intellectuals in Mexico, certainly the most important in promoting North American knowledge of Latin American literature and culture was the novelist and essayist Waldo Frank. I have chosen him as the protagonist of my first chapter. Not only did Frank embrace with unquestioning enthusiasm the cause of the Mexican Revolution, but, unlike most of his fellow countrymen, he spoke Spanish fluently. He established lasting friendships with Mexican intellectuals and ventured deeper than his compatriots into Latin

America. Inspired by the Mexican Revolution's celebration of the country's indigenous values, as well as by the Whitmanesque philosophy he had proclaimed in the magazine *The Seven Arts*, Frank put forward his theory of a "new world culture." Unlike Rodó, he believed the United States and Latin American intellectuals shared similar ideals and could bring about hemispheric spiritual renewal by forging a culture grounded in the American soil and respectful of mutual differences. In this program, Latin American regionalistic literature was destined to play an important role. It would acquaint Americans with the values of Hispanic culture, which Frank thought were closer to nature, and help them to recover their own lost links to the soil. Frank's program was unreasonably grandiose in scope; the dynamic inter-American exchange he sought would not be possible even today, despite the ease of travel and electronic communication. Nevertheless, he did succeed in making valuable contacts with authors throughout Latin America, in stirring up interest in U.S. culture there, and in pioneering the translation and diffusion of Latin American works in this country during the late twenties and thirties. Although his efforts had limited impact in the United States, in Latin America they helped turn prominent writers from reading exclusively European authors and point them toward some of the best America had to offer.

The second chapter of this study is an examination of Alfred A. Knopf and Blanche Knopf's efforts to make Americans aware of Latin American literature during the forties and fifties. The forties were a particularly promising time for Latin American writing in this country. Where Frank's crusade had only caught the attention of a small group of sympathetic intellectuals, President Franklin D. Roosevelt's Good Neighbor Policy developed an inter-American cultural exchange program of far-reaching impact. Interest in the languages and culture of Latin America became a matter of strategic importance for the United States during its war emergency. From the Office of the Coordinator of Inter-American Affairs, a federal agency designed to foster understanding between the Americas and to deter Nazi influence in the region, Nelson Rockefeller promoted language-study programs, cultural conferences, and the translation of works by Latin American authors. In order that literature coming out of Latin America might be easily available in the United States, financial support was provided to publishers who wanted to visit Latin America to view its literary scene and to those who printed translations of Spanish American or Brazilian writing. Among the most important books translated into English at the time were Ciro

Alegría's *Broad and Alien Is the World* (1941), published by Farrar and Rinehart; H. R. Hays's anthology *Twelve Spanish American Poets* (1943), published by Yale University Press; Dudley Fitts's *Anthology of Contemporary Latin American Poetry* (1942), published by New Directions; and Jorge Amado's *The Violent Land* (1945), published by Knopf.

Nowhere did the officially stimulated appetite for Hispanic books develop more vigorously than at Knopf's publishing house. As the Good Neighbor spirit waned with the end of the war, most New York publishers returned to Europe for their foreign books. Only Blanche and Alfred Knopf, and, to a lesser degree, James Laughlin at New Directions, continued to issue works by Latin authors. The Knopfs deserve great credit for making Americans aware of Latin American literature. Their publishing house was deeply committed to finding the broadest possible American audience for South American writers.

In the third chapter I focus on the little magazine *El Corno Emplumado/The Plumed Horn* and its role in disseminating Latin American poetry during the sixties. With the rise of the American "New Left," the counterculture, and the student movements during the sixties, interest in Latin America gained a new impetus. The Cuban Revolution was an important preoccupation for a large number of American anti-establishment artists and intellectuals who believed that Fidel Castro's experiment represented a humane version of communism in which artistic and political avant-gardes could coexist. Most of the editors of America's "little magazines" were in one way or another drawn to Cuba. *The Evergreen Review, Caterpillar, The Sixties,* and *El Corno Emplumado* are among the most prominent of the "littles" that made room for writing coming out of Latin America. Whereas Robert Bly's *The Sixties* brought readers the work of such world-renowned figures as Pablo Neruda and Cesar Vallejo, *El Corno Emplumado* took the lead in translating both established and new Latin American poets for American readers, and North American poetry for Spanish-speaking audiences. Edited in Mexico City by Margaret Randall and Sergio Mondragón, the publication forged strong ties with avant-garde groups in both hemispheres and developed a distinct inter-American perspective.

In the fourth and final chapter of this study I discuss the efforts of the Center for Inter-American Relations to draw attention to Latin American authors, especially novelists, during the late sixties and seventies. The publicity surrounding Castro's aggressive cultural policies in the early years of his rule is partly responsible for the vogue of Latin

American writing and art in Europe at the time. This "boom" of Latin American literature, as it has been called, arrived in the United States, in the late sixties, thanks to the Rockefeller-funded Center for Inter-American Relations. The center's literature program undertook the promotion of Spanish American and Brazilian authors on a grand scale. Its main goal was to once and for all establish Latin American writers as a marketable commodity in the United States. While *The Plumed Horn* catered to counterculture cliques, the center's targets were big publishers and nationally important publications like the *New York Times Book Review*, the *New York Review of Books*, *Time*, *Harper's*, and the *Atlantic*.

In this book I show how Latin American writers in the United States have moved from a position of almost complete invisibility to one of literary prominence. This is a story of setbacks and missed opportunities, as well as of triumphs. It is an account not only of the rise of particular literary reputations, but also of North American literary tastes, publishing, and hemispheric politics.

All translations of foreign quotes were done by me and are included in brackets.

NOTES

1. This study uses the words *American* and *North American* interchangeably; both terms refer to the United States of America.

2. Domingo Faustino Sarmiento, *Travels in the United States in 1847* (Princeton, NJ: Princeton University Press, 1970), 132.

3. José Martí, "Coney Island," in *Martí on the U.S.A.*, ed. Luis A. Baralt (Carbondale, IL: Southern Illinois University Press, 1966), 150.

4. Rubén Darío, "To Roosevelt," in *The Borzoi Anthology of Latin American Literature*, ed. Emir Rodríguez Monegal and Thomas Colchie (New York: Alfred A. Knopf, 1977), I: 357.

1

Waldo Frank's Crusade for Latin American Literature

Waldo Frank, who is now forgotten in Latin America, was once the most frequently read and admired North American author there. Though his work is largely neglected in the United States, he was at one time the leading North American expert on Latin American writing. His name looms large in tracing the careers of Latin American writers in this country before 1940. Long before Franklin D. Roosevelt launched the Good Neighbor policy, Frank brought back to his countrymen news of Latin American culture. Frank went to South America when he was almost forty. The youthful dreams of Frank and his fellow pre–World War I writers and artists to make their country a fit place for cultural renaissance that would change society had waned with the onset of the twenties.[1] But they had not completely vanished. Disgruntled by the climate of "normalcy" prevailing in America after World War I, he turned to Latin America. He started out in the Southwest. The remnants of Mexican culture he found in Arizona and New Mexico enticed him to venture further into the Hispanic world. In 1921 he traveled extensively in Spain, and in 1929 he spent six months exploring Latin America. While mainstream America showed him what he rejected—materialism and cultural conformity—Latin America represented a kind of organic society he hoped would eventually bloom at home. Latin America was a place, it seemed to him, where art and nature were closely intertwined. Latin America offered a way of life closer to the soil and the spirit—a way of life where the sense of community was central. It produced a literature that sustained these values. In the regionalistic writing popular in Latin America in the teens and twenties, writing that turned to the land and folklore for inspiration, he saw his Americanist aspirations realized. Moreover, Frank's messianic rhetoric and theory that a totally

new culture could emerge out of the Western Hemisphere suited well
the intellectual aspirations of his Latin hosts.[2]

In Frank's program to revitalize his own culture by making Americans aware of their southern neighbors' truer and more down-to-earth
values, Latin American literature played the leading part. Upon his return to the United States he embarked on a long-term project to draw
his countrymen's attention to Latin American regional writing. More
concerned with promoting literature that conveyed what he thought were
the essential traits of Latin America than with celebrating good writing,
he presented the American reader with a narrow view. Because his selection of which author to promote was determined by his Whitmanesque
ideals and unflagging Americanism, he was largely responsible for creating a stock image of Latin American letters as raw, colorful, passion-
ate, and of mainly anthropological interest.

I

In order to understand Frank's involvement with Latin America and its
writing, it is important to look at his background and relationship to
the American literary scene from about 1915. Like many other artists
and writers of his generation, Frank felt uneasy in his own culture. He
was especially bitter about America's puritan legacy, which he deemed
responsible for having suppressed art in favor of economic success. He
early tried expatriation to escape a culture he thought hostile to his ideals. Shortly after graduating from Yale in 1911, he left for Lausanne
where he studied philosophy. Later he drifted to Paris. There he spent
time with André Gide and other writers grouped around the *Nouvelle
Revue Française*. But Frank was one of the few American artists in
Paris who failed to find in Europe an antidote to the evils of American
civilization. Quite the opposite; it was in Paris that he started cultivat-
ing his bitterness and coming to terms with his culture.[3]

Upon his return to New York in 1916, he found in the loose coali-
tion of young artists and social critics known as the Lyrical Left or
Resurgents an echo of his personal and political aspirations. With Ran-
dolph Bourne, Van Wyck Brooks, and Alfred Stieglitz as its most
prominent leaders, these cultural radicals felt alienated from the materialistic orientation of American culture. They dreamed of bringing about
a revolution that would increase art's influence in society. As historian
Edward Abrahams has written: "[They] wanted to use art to liberate
themselves and society from what they considered to be artificial

abridgments of personal and social freedom. They proposed new, in-depth, psychological definitions of the self, a transcendental and antirational conception of the universe . . . a revolutionary socialist world order that, in their minds, stood for a new freedom for the individual and society."[4] The Resurgents worshipped Walt Whitman, who had called artists to a special mission. Like the poet, they wanted to create a new collective American consciousness. They believed that art should be rooted in American reality. Self-exploration and self-expression, they thought, could generate a new and more vital national culture.

Naturally attracted to the Lyrical Left's visionary project, Frank helped James Oppenheimer and Paul Rosenfeld create a journal that would promote cultural regeneration and a new Americanist spirit. *The Seven Arts*, as it was called, became the most important outlet for the Resurgents' program. It was in this magazine that Brooks called for the revival of romanticism's crusading spirit— "a warm, humane, concerted . . . revolutionary protest against whatever incubuses of crabbed age, paralysis, tyranny, stupidity, sloth, commercialism, lay most heavily upon the people's life."[5] Although some contributors were overtly socialist, the editors and most writers were simply extreme idealists who offered a redemptive vision of individual and communal liberation. On its pages we find the seeds of the ideas Frank later used to interpret Latin American culture. There is the French writer Romain Rolland's exhilaration with the newness of America: "You are free of traditions . . . you may go forward, unhampered to your future . . . your true model is within yourselves."[6] There is Frank's own assault on mechanistic America: "Our centers of civilization differ from those in Europe in this: that they are cities not so much of men and women as of buildings. The impervious structures that loom over us seem to blot us out."[7] And there is his approval of artists who used native materials and contempt for those who eschewed them: "There have been pure and deliberate visions among us. In art there has been Whistler; and Henry James took it into his head to write novels. But the clear subtlety of these men was achieved by a rigorous avoidance of native stuff and native issues; and their followers have done the same."[8]

October 1917 marked the end of *The Seven Arts*. The demise of the journal and American involvement in World War I meant for most members of the Lyrical Left the end of their hopes for a cultural revolution in the United States.[9] For Frank, however, the magazine was the start of a more ardent Americanist mission. *Our America* (1919), a work of cultural criticism designed to explain the United States to the

French, carried further the principles first formulated in the magazine. In the book, Frank rejected America's puritan legacy and present materialism. Instead, he hoped for a utopian future based on the simpler, organic values of a pre-industrial past. Indeed, his work expresses what cultural historian Peter Conn has identified as the central dialectic of American culture in the opening decades of this century, that is, "the conflict between tradition and innovation, between control and independence, between order and liberation."[10] The puritan-hating intellectuals of the 1920s hailed the book as the ultimate truth. The study also foreshadowed Frank's future fascination with Latin America. In chapter 4, "The Land of Buried Cultures," which he wrote after a brief stay in the Southwest, he focused on Mexican Americans. His interpretation of their way of life laid the groundwork of his theory of the "Two American Half Worlds," later developed in his writings about Latin America. The Mexicans' closeness to nature and mystic religion, he thought, would make up for the lack of spirituality of mainstream American culture: "The true marriage of the Indian and the Spaniard has brought about a native culture. The lowly Mexican is articulate, the lordly American is not. For the Mexican has really dwelt with his soil, cultivated his spirit in it, not alone his maize."[11]

This section caught the attention of Latin American intellectuals long before Frank decided to visit South America. For example, Juan José Tablada, a Mexican poet and journalist living in New York in 1922, read it as an expression of sympathy for downtrodden Mexican Americans. Tablada reminded his readers in *Excelsior* that though Frank was not alone—there were also Theodore Dreiser, Sherwood Anderson, and William Carlos Williams—he was the unquestionable leader of a new generation of writers who rebelled against Babbitry.[12] Elsewhere in Latin America, socialists made use of *Our America* to protest U.S. leadership in the hemisphere. Argentine socialist Alfredo Palacios chose to translate Frank's harshest criticism of his country to show his readers that America was "culturally sick"[13] and that even sensitive North Americans detested their culture.

Less reductive was José Carlos Mariátegui's appraisal of the book in Peru. In 1925 he published "Waldo Frank" in the *Boletín Bibliográfico* of the University of San Marcos in Lima. The article commended Frank's portrayal of America and discussed Frank's philosophy in general. As critic Arnold Chapman has observed, Mariátegui's reading was more enlightened because it held that "to reject the United States out of hand . . . would be a simplistic error which would throw away a very real chance to join forces with enlightened elements in Yanquilandia. Thus he becomes the first Hispanic writer really to understand Frank's concept of the creative minority."[14]

At home *Our America* was quite a success. Kenneth Burke went so far as to list it among the books that "had changed our minds."[15] Frank's vogue was short-lived. His next books and his insistence on carrying the Resurgent spirit into the 1920s were rapidly dismissed by his colleagues in New York and Paris. As Malcolm Cowley retrospectively noted, the Resurgents "gathered about the great unhappy body of the nation, they laid their spells upon it and adjured it to labor intellectually and bring forth a native American culture. When the baby was born many of the doctors were looking the other way."[16] Indeed, to a generation embittered by the war, which relished Dada's outrageous experiments and was haunted by the glum intonations of T. S. Eliot's *The Wasteland* (1922), Frank's messianic outpourings meant little. For example, Matthew Josephson, editor of the Dadaist periodical *Broom*, had no patience with Frank. When critic Gorham Munson tried to insist on having *Broom* publish a eulogy of Frank and his work, Josephson flatly refused. He also dismissed Frank's *City Block* (1922), a novel about New York slums, as wordy and irrelevant. Years later Josephson would sheepishly regret his youthful irreverence: "I now realize in anger and repentance that instead of trying to amuse myself and my readers by parodying Frank's overblown style and deriding his messianic ideas about sexual freedom and the New Dawn I might have chided him with a kindlier humor."[17]

A change in intellectual enthusiasms in the United States explains the poor recognition Frank received for his work after *Our America*. In the 1920s, as historian Richard Pells has observed, "The union between culture and politics began visibly to disintegrate. . . . Those who tried to . . . create a viable radical movement in the United States were wasting their talents and energy. . . . [Artists and social critics] redefined their roles on 'a somewhat narrower basis.' "[18]

Despite his recognized talent and versatility, he remained largely, as Maxwell Geismar wrote, "a prophet without honor in his own country."[19] Neglected at home and feeling that only in Latin America could he find fertile ground to cultivate his theories, Frank was compelled to travel south of the Río Grande in the late 1920s.

II

Having discovered in the Southwest a spirituality absent in American culture, Frank went to Spain in 1921 to look for its origins. The outcome of his Spanish experience was another cultural portrait, *Virgin Spain* (1926), which in turn later motivated his visit to Latin America. While Frank was working on his book in the mid-twenties, he met Alfonso Reyes, Mexico's leading essayist, who encouraged him to explore Latin America. In the preface to the second Spanish-language edition of *Virgin Spain*, Reyes wrote: "Natural que, viendo a Waldo tan interesado en España—lo que ya era para mí de muy buen augurio—se me ocurriera decirle: 'No olvides que España es el camino para nuestra América.' " [Evidently, when I realized that Waldo was so interested in Spain—which for me was good sign—I told him: "Do not forget that Spain points the way to our America."][20]

And so it proved for Frank. With the Spanish writers known as the "Generation of 1898," he conceived of Spanish culture as separate from that of the rest of Europe. The vision he took from the Spanish intellectuals' mystique of Spain emphasized that their culture was more medieval and more organic than German, British, or French culture. It differed from the rest of the continent because it had been affected more deeply by Oriental and African influences. Like the former colonies in the Southwest, Spanish culture was animated by a collective spirit and closeness to the land that departed radically from the individualistic essence of industrial Europe. In Spain, Frank found what he wanted. He later confessed in his *Memoirs* how it happened: "One day as I strolled down one of the new avenues . . . I got the sudden answer to my love of Spain. The average Spaniard was an integrated person. In the Western peoples, from central Europe to the United States, the immense pressures and invasions of modern science—the machine—have alienated man from his instinctual counterpoint with his earth, his group, and his self. Man always seeks a whole to live in."[21]

The organic quality of Spanish life did not prevent him, however, from seeing its shortcomings. While extolling the Spaniard's natural dignity and ability to integrate individual with communal goals, he believed Spain's strong attachment to a feudal past had thwarted its cultural growth. He felt in Spain an absence of energy, a "dark and stagnant mood";[22] he believed Spain represented a "dead or failed civilization."[23]

In the United States *Virgin Spain* did not fare well. The most recurrent term used by New York reviewers to describe it was *travelogue*. Moreover, critics seem to have been prevented from taking the work seriously by the excesses of Frank's style, as for instance in his description of Seville:

This fixity, this intricate appearance within fixity is the deep trait of Seville. Her genius, her emotions, her religion are in fixity for they are held unwavering to herself. She looks not at Spain nor the world. Not like Venus does this goddess walk and give herself to men. Not like Astarte, thirst for the blood of others. Not like Isis is she concerned with the cycles of sun and planet. Seville loves only herself; and the moon and stars are brilliant for her hair. The narcissism of Seville is fecund. The gorgeous litany of the Semana Santa is but the most famous of her arts. Religion is but the most obvious pretext of her self-worship. Seville abounds in dramas and in altars of her self-delight.[24]

While U.S. critics were upset by what they deemed Frank's "inability to restrain himself,"[25] in Latin America the book scored a great success just for that reason. Readers were enthralled by Frank's tendency to dramatize rather than coolly analyze his subject. His ornate imagery was also appealing for its resemblance to Latin American poetic prose like that of Darío or Rodó. The reviewers were flattering. To Federico de Onís, chairman of the Spanish Department at Columbia, it was "the most moving book that any foreigner has ever written about Spain."[26] Chilean journalist Ernesto Montenegro was completely won over by its flamboyant style: "We find him at his best when . . . he abandons himself to his keen poetic intuition."[27] For Latin Americans *Virgin Spain* was no travel book, but a carefully drawn portrait of their mother culture.

Pleased by his warm reception, Frank hastened his plans to visit Latin America. In 1926 he set out for Cuba and the Isle of Pines with his friend and protégé Hart Crane. Inspired by his sojourn in Spain, he was determined to make of this short vacation a recapitulation of the experience of self-discovery he had undergone there. In Cuba he found the same small town neighborliness of the mother country, the same "fire" in its people. But he thought the Cubans had mellowed their heritage: "The rigor of Spain has swooned beneath the sun and blossomed again into the ease of Cuba."[28] It is interesting to compare Frank's romanticized vision with Crane's reaction. Though influenced by the "soil values" Frank had exalted in *The Seven Arts*, Crane was not able

to share his friend's enthusiasm. In a letter to his father he described
Havana as "a funny little metropolis . . . and more like a toy city than
a real one. The Cubans seem such trashy, bastard people—without any
sense of direction or purpose. We enjoyed the tobacco, however, and the
Bacardi."[29]

The aura of excitement that surrounded Mexico in the late 1920s encouraged Frank to begin his long Latin American tour in that country.
In 1929, Mexicans were still living off of the revolutionary dreams that
had lured so many American artists and writers. Though for many the
revolution had failed to fulfill its promise, Frank encountered a sizable
American colony still enamored of Mexican art and cultural vitality.
Among them were his friends William Spratling, who revived the sil-
versmith craft in Taxco, the writer Anita Brenner, and the anthropologist Stuart Chase.

Frank rapidly attuned himself to the mood of his friends. He realized
that Mexico had become a second Paris, a place one could go to escape
the platitudes of American individualism and industrial blight. Paris offered culture and sophistication; Mexico mystery and closeness to "the
origins." Its "certain rawness," its "mongrel quality" reminded Americans of D. H. Lawrence's maxim in his essay "America, Listen to Your
Own": "Catch the spirit of your own, dark, aboriginal continent, and
take up life where the Red Indian, the Aztec, the Maya left it off."[30]
Furthermore, it offered the opportunity to participate simultaneously in
a millennial culture and a progressive revolution. The fusion of art and
politics satisfied the wildest dreams of American socialists, pacifists,
and bohemians. As journalist Carleton Beals put it, Mexico represented
a moving force of human betterment: more education, land for the peasants, "an upsurge of new writing, literature, art, music with no attempt
to squeeze it . . . into one little green tub of intolerance."[31]

Nothing could have been more stimulating for Frank than the intellectual climate he encountered in Mexico. An ardent believer in national
consciousness, he marveled at the Mexicans' passion for art, their interest in personal relations, and their attachment to their roots. He shared
Edward Weston's attraction to the "elemental expression"[32] of the peasants and Crane's awe over their "unmechanized, immediate"[33] economy.
In a lecture entitled "The New World" delivered in Spanish at the
Universidad Autónoma in Mexico City, Frank took a step further than
his American colleagues. He invited Mexican intellectuals to join their
counterparts in the United States in a program of cultural renaissance.
Thousands of students heard him in the main plaza of the campus. The

leading paper devoted its main editorial to the lecture and vigorously endorsed his program. "We accept the invitation, the challenge, the collaboration,"[34] read its opening lines.

Frank's New World rhetoric was particularly appealing to the local artists and intellectuals. He shared their nonmaterialistic, and pro-communal views of life and culture. He harped on topics Mexicans never tired of discussing. Like his Mexican audience, he criticized "the evils of American business." He compared the suffering of the artist in the United States to the lot of the peasants of Tampico controlled by the Yankee "kingdoms of oil."[35]

The intellectual discovery of Mexico prompted him to probe deeper into the Latin American continent. While Crane, Porter, and other Americans assured Mexicans that the world was interested in their culture, Frank was bent on extending this interest to all of South America. Like his friend Alfred Stieglitz at home, he saw himself as a spiritual and intellectual leader whose mission was to spark hemispheric revolution based on personal freedom and cultural renewal.

Frank's journey to South America was viewed in the context of the time as something extraordinary. South Americans had fewer contacts with American intellectuals than Mexicans did. Whereas in Mexico he had been received as a prophet, in Buenos Aires and the rest of South America he was treated as something more important, a great writer. Accustomed to indifference at home, Frank was amazed by the Argentines' lavish welcome. Argentine writers were already familiar with his ideas. In 1929 Frank had sent through Alfonso Reyes a message to Mexican intellectuals, which was published in Argentine journals. Before he completed his stay in Argentina, he was bombarded by invitations to lecture at Chilean, Uruguayan, Colombian, Peruvian, and Cuban universities. Moreover, leading newspapers like *La Nación* and *La Prensa* asked him to become a regular contributor.

Considering the obstacles that lay before him, Frank's instant communion with his South American audience was quite a feat. To begin with, he had to contend with a generation of intellectuals, who, though supportive of his brand of Americanism, had grown up reading Darío and Rodó. Tinged by Arielismo, their vision of the United States was that of a pragmatic, materialistic culture where art was nonexistent. Their traditional orientation toward Europe hardened them against anything coming from the north. Frank's lectures, later collected in *Primer mensaje a la América Hispana* (1930) and published only in Spanish, set out to change these biases.

Notwithstanding his own reservations, Frank tried to show his hosts
that the United States could legitimately boast of a rich cultural life.
The lectures carefully outlined the development of American literature
and talked eloquently of, among others, Whitman, Melville, and
Frank's contemporary William Carlos Williams. He also introduced his
audiences to the work of his beloved Alfred Stieglitz and Isadora Duncan. His lectures created a new image of the United States among Latin
American intellectuals. As critic M. J. Benardete noted in 1930: "The
deep thoughts of Royce on loyalty, the liberalizing concepts of San-
tayana on the Life of Reason, the tumbling uncertainties of soul in
search and travail like that of Henry Adams . . . the unique paintings
of Georgia O'Keefe and John Marin, —such positive achievements as
these in art, philosophy and life which are making the culture of this
country, were up to the time of Waldo Frank's trip, a closed book to
these minorities of South America."[36] The lectures also expanded on
his theory of the two American half-worlds. The American continent,
he argued, was made up of a mercantile, industrialized, and politically
more successful United States and of the still feudal, agrarian but more
spiritual Latin American nations. Together they could forge a new culture.

Though at times Frank sounded like Rodó in his dismissal of his
own culture and his stress on the "purer" quality of Latin American life,
he was not uncritical of the culture of his hosts. For him, Latin America was as deeply in chaos as the United States. The spiritual values in-
herited from Spain had yet to take root. With his usual messianic ardor,
Frank called on intellectuals to realize the promise of their spiritual heritage.

Frank did not permit Latin Americans to blame the United States for
all of their problems: "Es tan fácil decir que los Estados Unidos son el
enemigo . . . y tan fácil recluirse en el olvido de la propia insuficien-
cia." [It is so easy to say that the United States is the enemy . . . so
easy to forget our own weaknesses.][37] Comments like that sparked
lively debates rather than anger in his hosts. From Communists to
Catholics, few remained indifferent to his message. In Havana the magazine *Avance* commended the honesty of his opinions about the existing intellectual atmosphere. In Lima, José Carlos Mariátegui and critic
Luis Alberto Sánchez applauded his views on the social role of the
American writers. As well as appreciating his lofty speeches, Latin
Americans, like critic Benardete, were seduced by his candor: "The
North American writer's eagerness to speak Spanish is praisewor-

thy. . . . Hitherto, foreign lecturers have not condescended to speak Spanish, not for anything in the world; it seemed to them that it violated their personality. In this the most disdainful were the French, who believed that the whole world was obliged to know French."[38]

Frank's broad knowledge of Latin American culture was equally appreciated. Cultured benefactress of the arts Victoria Ocampo contrasted Frank with diplomatic envoys who toured South America in the late thirties and forties: "Donald Francis, mandado por estos parajes por Nelson Rockefeller, me pareció lo más parado en la loma, lo que ustedes llaman dumbbell. Es realmente estúpido que envíen a un señor que no entiende una palabra de español." [Donald Francis, sent down here by Nelson Rockefeller, seemed really out of it, what you call a dumbbell. It is really stupid to send a gentleman who can not understand a word of Spanish.][39]

Frank's impressions of Latin American culture were collected in *América Hispana: South of Us* (1930). As he had done for Spain in *Virgin Spain*, he drew up a cultural portrait of South America. Latin America is seen as a primeval force, an all-enveloping setting that calls to mind the mythical New World in William Carlos Williams's *In the American Grain* (1925).

In Frank's Latin America, culture is an expression of nature. His reading emphasizes the region's mythical geography and neglects human achievement. Argentine critic Juan José Sebreli, a Marxist, contends that Frank and other mystical Americanists like German Hermann von Keyserling and Argentine essayist Ezequiel Martínez Estrada naturalized events that are essentially historical.[40]

In Peru, for example, Frank perceived culture as an expression of the Indians' relationship with the rocky and "elemental" Andes. The section devoted to Argentina and Uruguay has the pampa for a central motif. Its vastness and the motion of the grass have molded Argentine thought. Like the Andean Indian, the Argentine gaucho embodies the values of the land. In Brazil, man has become one with the forest and lives "entextured in the looming trees."[41]

In the United States the book suffered a fate similar to that of *Virgin Spain*. Few critics reviewed it. Its publisher, Sam Sloan, dismally reported to Frank: "The rate of sale . . . is enough to make me weep."[42] In 1943, Frank wrote a revised version, which included his experiences as a Good Neighbor envoy. His hopes of benefiting from the prevalent inter-American spirit rapidly vanished when he learned that *South American Journey* had fared even worse than its earlier version.

As before, Frank found consolation in Latin America, where he claimed his books found the "acceptance of the best minds."[43] Their tone and content suited well the Americanist spirit pervading Latin American letters at the time. They blended perfectly with the spirit of such works as Mariátegui's *Siete ensayos de interpretación de la realidad peruana* (1928) and Ricardo Rojas's *Eurindia* (1924). *América Hispana* also anticipated such seminal studies of Latin America as *The Masters and the Slaves* (1933) by Brazilian Gilberto Freyre and *Radiografía de la pampa* (1933) by Ezequiel Martínez Estrada.

III

Throughout the twenties and thirties Frank was an avid reader of Latin American literature. In the late twenties Latin American novelists had experienced their own version of Resurgence. Like cultural radicals in the United States, they too thought art could shake the foundations of the world. With Frank they cherished a New World literature that would cast Europe aside and accordingly turned to local customs and landscapes for inspiration. This literary nationalism, which gloried in writing and art that used regional linguistic expressions and indulged in local color, caught Frank's fancy. Latin authors' advocacy of novels as agents of Americanization and social change revived a faith in the power of art that he had lost in his country. As he noted: "They go, for their material, to life itself. And they instinctively form their material, so as to make it accessible (like the great novelists of England, France, Russia) to a large audience. . . . The contemporary Spanish American fiction is characterized by two outstanding traits: its variety and its vitality."[44]

Frank's criteria for determining literary quality sat well with Latin American critics, though they now seem simplistic. He favored subject matter over language, literal transcription over imaginative presentation of reality. Where William Carlos Williams believed that a new American literature entailed a "new method" with its "own rules,"[45] Frank thought the setting itself could be relied upon to provide the renewal: "The writers of the 'colonial period' were repressed: rigid Spanish and Catholic traditions kept them from immediate contact with the stupendously rich and luxuriant life of these wonderful countries . . . and now it's as if all the tropical splendor, all the mountainous energy of this varied world . . . had suddenly burst with flaming articulation. The Spanish American novelist . . . has gone at last to the native soil and has brought forth treasures."[46]

Closeness to nature and a supportive social environment, he pointed out, had much to do with the flourishing of poetic genius in Latin America. Unlike the Anglo-American tradition, he considered the Spanish and Catholic heritage more respectful of the arts, for it "impregnated the people with that tragic sense of life, inherent in all great art, which our sleazy eighteenth- and nineteenth-century optimism rubbed out . . . and prepares the mind to conceive life as organic and whole."[47] The only thing lacking in this happy state of the arts was adequate promotion abroad. And this Frank made it a goal to achieve.

He had taken on a difficult task. Before 1930 only a handful of Latin American books had been translated into English. The novel *María* (1867) by Colombian Jorge Isaacs and Rodó's *Ariel*, which were translated in 1918 and 1922 respectively, had barely made an impact.

To judge by the attitude of Colombian novelist José Eustasio Rivera and other aspiring writers, Frank was viewed as an arbiter of taste, an influential critic who could seriously promote their work in this country. In a letter to Frank, Rivera in 1928 coyly asked for endorsement of his forthcoming "jungle novel," *The Vortex:* "¿A propósito, leyó usted mi obrilla?" [By the way, have you read my little novel?][48] The English version did not appear until 1935 and elicited little interest.

The first Latin American novel officially supported by Frank was Mariano Azuela's *The Underdogs*, published in 1929. To make a case for this novel was easier than for many other Latin American works. The Mexican Revolution was a phenomenon that continued to interest American intellectuals. Moreover, in the late 1920s the presence of Mexican muralists in New York and Los Angeles had kept enthusiasm for art coming from Mexico very much alive.[49]

Frank wrote a glowing review of *The Underdogs* for *The New Republic*. To set it in its right context, he paired his appraisal with a commentary on Anita Brenner's cultural history of Mexico, *Idols Behind Altars* (1929). Brenner, who had considered translating the novel herself, was a close friend of Frank. Though more interested in Mexico's pre-Columbian heritage than in its Spanish roots, she shared Frank's passion for Latin American art.

Frank considered Azuela's novel to be the best example of the cultural renaissance brought about by the revolution. He felt it was a genuine New World book because of its native characters and situations. Unfortunately, Frank overlooked the aesthetic value of Azuela's book. Though he briefly alluded to its deft use of colloquial Spanish, he disregarded its cinematic narrative technique, which pioneered modernism in

Latin America. From Frank's review the American reader could only conclude that the Mexican writer was merely a mouthpiece for the revolution: "You may admit that no man could record so low a story and make it beautiful, who was not a great man. I prefer to insist that no man could have done this who did not belong to a potentially great people."[50]

Frank was equally enthusiastic about Azuela's second novel, published in English by Farrar and Rinehart in 1932. *Marcela: A Mexican Love Story*, a conventional romantic novel, was translated by Brenner while she traveled through Spain in 1930. Frank followed her woes over the translation very closely and later wrote a flattering introduction. The novel matched Frank's view of Latin American literature. Its documentary mode conveyed moral outrage at social injustice and depicted local customs. More than a love story, the novel struck him as a study of class conflict: "*Marcela* . . . is a class-conscious melodrama. . . . It is a portrait—accurate, racy, true—of Mexican life; of that depth of Mexican life which revolution has not really altered. Here, the reader will experience something of the mysterious soul of the Indian peasant. . . . And here also are the pious ladies of wealth . . . the dissolute sons . . . against whom the peasants of Madero and Zapata rose."[51]

Because the thirties were a propitious time for socialism and protest art in the United States, Brenner and Frank had high expectations for the novel. But few reviewers agreed with their assessment. Ignoring the political overtones, the reviewers discounted it as a "stirring little tale."[52] Only Peggy Baird, Malcolm Cowley's estranged wife, shared Frank's excitement. As with Frank, the book's murky language and stock characters were outweighed in her mind by Azuela's detailed rendering of Mexican life.[53]

As for writers from deeper in Latin America, Frank found himself quite alone. With the exception of Spanish professors like Isaac Goldberg and Federico de Onís, there were very few writers and even fewer publishers who had any interest in Latin American literature. This did not discourage him. He seemed to have liked seeing himself as a prophet striving alone for a neglected literature.

To account for the authors he chose to endorse, one must delve into his friendships with writers throughout South America. Among the most influential was Argentine Samuel Glüsberg, better known by his pseudonym Enrique Espinoza. Ever since Glüsberg had read *Our America* in 1921, he had followed Frank's career closely. He had started but never finished a translation of Frank's novel *Holiday* (1923). He sent Frank a copy of his short story collection *La levita gris* (1924). Frank was so impressed that he translated one of the stories, "The Cross," and published it in *The Menorah Journal* in 1926. Because of the Jewish journal's limited circulation, the story left no imprint. Nevertheless, it is typical of Frank's long infatuation with Latin American letters. In 1929 Glüsberg arranged Frank's first visit to Buenos Aires.[54]

When Frank returned to New York in 1930, he became an editorial advisor for Latin American letters at Doubleday, Doran and Company. Despite his good intentions, he was never to be successful at that publishing company. It is interesting, however, to see what he had in mind. As he explained in a message delivered to Latin American writers: "I am going to do what I can to make known the creative spirit of your America to the readers of my America. . . . The interest in Latin American culture has almost entirely to be created. . . . We shall have to judge books not alone from the standpoint of their intrinsic literary value, but as well from that of their portrayal of American life. . . . For my motive is to help my America understand your America."[55]

Just as in *The Seven Arts* he had discarded the "un-American" Whistler and James, as a Doubleday advisor he overlooked Latin American avant-gardists. He focused instead on works that were closer to folklore than to what Latin Americans themselves considered to be high literature. One of the projects at Doubleday included publishing a collection of Peruvian short tales. As his chief in-country assistant, he chose his friend and ardent Americanist critic Luis Alberto Sánchez. The book was to be structured along the lines of *América Hispana*. By setting the tales in their geographic and historical setting, Frank wanted to create a cultural map of Peru through its literature. The collection was to include Abraham Valdelomar's allegorical stories of the coastal region. Life in the Andes would be portrayed by an Indian story of Enrique López Albújar. One of Ricardo Palma's spicy "tradiciones" was to convey the flavor of colonial Lima. From a literary standpoint, the selection could only have reinforced the prevailing notion of Latin American literature as provincial, local color writing.[56]

There are no documents to explain what became of the Doubleday, Doran project. It apparently foundered quickly. By late 1930 Frank had become the editorial advisor for the new Farrar and Rinehart Latin American series. John Farrar, the publisher, had great hopes for it. "We intend," he wrote, "to pursue this through the years with the most reasonable profits for all concerned."[57] Frank's first assignment was to edit a volume of Argentine short stories. His main consultant was Glüsberg, who shared his admiration for traditional gauchesque literature and documentary writing. Like many South American authors at the time, Frank was intrigued by rural life. He wanted to excite in American readers the same awe he felt about the pampas. Glüsberg suggested *El ombú* (1902) by the English writer W. Henry Hudson as the best depiction of life in the Argentine countryside: "No hay nada igual sobre el campo argentino" [Nothing like it has been written about the Argentine countryside], he said. He also enlisted Frank's support for Roberto Payró's picaresque and socially critical sketches and for a selection from classic gauchesque literature by Benito Lynch or Ricardo Güiraldes. Glüsberg suggested that he concentrate on earlier authors: "Quizás para no quedar mal con nadie le convenga más poner en un volumen tres historias de tres autores muertos: Hudson, Payró y Güiraldes." [To avoid problems it would be better to publish in one volume three stories of dead authors: Hudson, Payró, and Güiraldes.][58]

Originally Frank had planned to translate the stories himself, but he later turned them over to Brenner, who had a better command of the Spanish language. With the exception of W. Henry Hudson, whom he thought too attached to the Old World, he followed Glüsberg's advice closely. He included "Laucha's Marriage" and "The Devil in Pago Chico" by Roberto Payró. Before his death in 1928, Payró had expressed the wish to have Frank himself translate his work.[59] Though his wish was not fulfilled, he would have been pleased to learn that he was the only author to have two stories in a volume that included such prominent names as Sarmiento and Güiraldes. The emphasis was on the classics. Among them was an excerpt from Sarmiento's *Facundo* (1845), Güiraldes's "Rosaura," and Leopoldo Lugones's Americanistic "Death of a Gaucho." Of all the stories, "The Return of the Anaconda" by Uruguayan Horacio Quiroga was the most modern. Quiroga has often been compared to Edgar Allan Poe. His penchant for the Gothic and preoccupation with the art of the short story shows—as critic Jean Franco wrote—that he was aware of the limitations of regionalism.[60]

In the preface to the book, Frank stressed content over literary skill. He hoped the tales would acquaint Americans with Argentine culture: "The Argentine eye ... is an essentialisation of the pampa.... There are no sharp colors in the country.... Yet in this lack of accentuated form and color, Argentina has a profound savor of fecundity.... The same unassertive fecundity exists in the sprawling literature of Argentina."[61]

Reviewers followed Frank's lead. For the most part, they disregarded the aesthetic value of the stories. Margaret Wallace in the *New York Times* acknowledged the informative purpose of the volume and then proceeded to discount the stories as ethnic sketches not worth much attention.[62] Only Harriet de Onís, a translator of Latin American writing herself, took the trouble to look at the tales more closely.[63] Despite the mixed reviews, the book fared reasonably well. Encouraged by the sales figures—4,000 copies—Farrar believed the Latin American publishing project was bound to do "highly spectacular and rather luxurious things."[64]

Frank thought that the best literature in Latin America was being written in Argentina. In a sense, he was right. Argentine writing offered the most diversity. There was a strong nativist tradition as well as daring avant-garde groups, which in the twenties had been busy—as the editors of the newspaper *Martín Fierro* maintained—inventing new metaphors and assimilating "everything new under the sun."[65] Frank admired the Argentine authors' mastery of the techniques of the short story and considered them fated to excel as "a literary people, . . . even as Mexico and Peru are essentially plastic nations."[66]

Given the performance of *Tales*, Farrar undertook the publication of *Don Segundo Sombra* (1926) by Ricardo Güiraldes. This classic of gauchesque literature was the perfect choice. The tone and content of the novel were unmistakably Americanist. Life in the pampa and the feats of its native inhabitant, the gaucho, were lyrically described. Yet, despite Güiraldes's copious use of indigenous terms, the novel did not smack of the provincial. As most critics agreed, the book moves beyond the rigid scope of regionalism onto a mythic level.

Don Segundo Sombra had been a smashing success in Spain and Latin America. In France it had sparked an interest that was unprecedented for a novel coming out of a Hispanic country.[67] Güiraldes's widow, Adelina, would recall readers' exuberant response in a letter she wrote to Frank: "Fue un éxito ruidoso al que escapó escondiéndose en 'La Porteña.' " [It was a roaring success, which he eluded by hiding at his ranch, "La Porteña."][68]

Most likely, Victoria Ocampo first encouraged Frank to read *Don Segundo Sombra*. Through her, he had met Güiraldes, visited his farm, and seen him playing the gaucho. In addition to Americanist elements, the book appealed to Frank for its lyrical dimension. The author's musing on the silence of the pampa reminded Frank of his own raptures over that landscape: "I breathed deeply of the breath of the sleeping

fields. It was a calm darkness gladdened with shining patches of light
like sparks of a noisy fire."[69] He may have also been drawn to the
mystical aura the book exuded. Like Frank, Güiraldes was interested in
mysticism and Eastern religions, and he despised modern mechaniza-
tion. And, like Frank, he saw in the machine a threat to rural and more
communal forms of existence.

Frank's intention was to have Brenner translate the novel. After she
declined, believing she was not "well enough informed to do the book
justice,"[70] Frank resorted to Harriet de Onís. She and her husband Federico gladly accepted the job and promised to work on *Don Segundo*
"con todo amor y cariño" [with love and care].[71]

The outcome of the de Onís's efforts did not satisfy Frank. He felt
their translation had robbed the original of its lyrical quality and produced a bland, flat narrative. Feeling responsible for the fate of anything
involving Latin America, he rewrote their English version: "I did *Don
Segundo Sombra*'s translation because my conscience forced me
to. . . . This book is an exquisite one, I have for a year been trying to
patch it up, but its rhythm was wrong. So I gritted my teeth and entirely rewrote it in less than three weeks."[72]

The problems of the translation were but one of the first obstacles the
novel faced in this country. Frank's lofty ideals were ill-suited to the
practicalities of publishing. When Farrar decided to replace the original
Spanish title and launch the English version as *Shadows in the Pampas*, Frank came close to resigning his job: "I am responsible for this
book. . . . I am shocked beyond measure . . . the book must be called
Don Segundo Sombra."[73] Elsewhere, he accused Farrar of crass commercialism: "I have no doubt that you were urged to make this change
by your selling force who probably told you that it was difficult to
place a novel called *Don Segundo Sombra*."[74]

The dispute reached a climax when Farrar postponed the book's re-
lease and took it off the spring list of 1934. The impasse was resolved
when both Frank and the publisher agreed to consult with Adelina Güiraldes in Buenos Aires. She called the translation a "tour de force"[75] and
suggested a Solomonic compromise. The novel finally appeared as *Don
Segundo Sombra: Shadow in the Pampas* in 1935. Looking back, it
seems that Farrar's judgment had some validity. A public that was un-
familiar with Latin America, largely isolationist or European-oriented,
would naturally feel at a loss when faced with a novel titled in Spanish.

In the introduction to the novel Frank tried to make the work more
familiar to American readers. He banked on the book's solid French

success and stressed how close its narrative pattern was to that of the American frontier novel. In the portrayal of life beyond the settlement, he argued, *Don Segundo* recalled Huck Finn: "It, too, is the history of a boy, a waif who 'on his own' wanders through the country. And that country, in both books, is the frontier—an old America that had already almost vanished when the two books were written."[76] When he analyzed the differences between the two novels, he drew on his theory of the "two American half worlds." He conveniently set aside the indigenous origins of the gaucho, emphasized his Spanish, Catholic heritage, and extolled his innate nobility.[77] Huck, instead, was the offspring of a "barbarous, anarchic America where the traditions of Old England are broken up past recognition."[78]

Quite a few reviewers noticed the appearance of *Don Segundo*. The *Nation* assigned Anita Brenner to comment on it. She praised it lavishly and echoed Frank's reading of the book: "Unmistakably this is an American book. . . . It has the feel of space, endless and generous and dangerous . . . the enormous hopefulness of the primitive."[79] Fred T. Marsh's appraisal in the *New York Times Book Review* acknowledged the book's universal appeal. Marsh reinforced its similarities with the Spanish picaresque tradition and U.S. frontier writing and maintained that its "Argentiness" was worthy of no more than passing attention.[80] In the *Saturday Review of Literature*, the reviewer failed to account for the poetry of some episodes. In his opinion, *Don Segundo* was nothing but an exotic dime novel: "The narrator . . . goes through a series of adventures which give the reader a pretty complete notion of bronco-busting and cattle-driving in the Argentine."[81] If in France *Don Segundo* had started a change of critical attitude toward Latin American literature, in this country it had merely whetted the appetite for the picturesque and discouraged more serious and formal readings.[82]

With *Don Segundo*, José Hernández's *Martín Fierro* (1872) was the Latin American work Frank loved most. He shared the author's distrust of institutions and progress and saw the epic as a spontaneous outgrowth of the Argentine people. Years before the book appeared in English, Frank had called it, in *América Hispana*, the "greatest folk poem of the modern Western World."[83]

Frank's murky description of *Martín Fierro* as rising from the "ripe depths of Catholic Europe . . . transfigured by the rhythms . . . of America"[84] had little in common with the strong, earthy language Hernández used in Spanish. It was difficult to find a translator. Joseph Ausslander had translated the first twenty-six cantos and published them in *Hispanic Notes* in 1932. But the length of the poem had dissuaded him from continuing with the translation. Frank chose to work with Walter Owen's free translation published in England in 1935. Owen's version included a set of notes explaining regional vocabulary and customs to English-speaking readers.

From a commercial standpoint *Martín Fierro* proved to be, as Farrar noted, "an even more difficult problem" than *Don Segundo*.[85] Critically, however, it received wider recognition. Yet, as with *Don Segundo*, critics barely mentioned its literary merits and universal appeal. By failing to comment on Hernández's masterful characterization of his hero and on his humor, critics reduced it to another sample of exotica, a piece of ethnic literature, and nothing else.[86]

After *Martín Fierro*'s feeble sales—less than 2,000 copies—the Farrar Latin American series retreated from its original goals. Translations of works by Argentine Leopoldo Lugones, Venezuelans Rufino Blanco-Fombona and Teresa de la Parra, and Cuban novelist Alfonso Hernández-Catá never materialized. Though *Doña Barbara* (1929), by Venezuelan Rómulo Gallegos, and *The Vortex* (1924) were issued by rival publishers, few Latin American books found their way into English before the forties. The only Latin American work Frank dealt with after the late thirties was the novel *Dom Casmurro* (1900) by Brazilian Joaquim María Machado de Assis. Frank wrote the introduction for the English translation published by Noonday Press in 1953.

The outcome of Frank's editorial adventure was not as successful as he had hoped. Aside from the scant interest in Latin America existing at the time, his criteria of selection hindered a better response. Had he chosen to balance his heavily Americanist list with works of more universal appeal, the story of Latin American literature in this country might have been different. Like the United States during the 1920s, Latin America had more to offer than the prevailing taste for regionalism in literature. In Peru, César Vallejo had revolutionized Spanish American poetry while keeping alive the social and political dimensions Frank thought to be an essential part of literature. As early as 1933 the little magazine *Megáfono* had devoted a full issue to Jorge Luis Borges's work and acknowledged his influence on a new generation of writers.[87] Yet, it seems that Frank avoided anything that did not overtly deal with American landscape and folklore. In *South American Journey* Frank called Borges "his generation's finest stylist," but he criticized him for "brazenly [devoting] his genius to a literature of fantasy and utter escape."[88]

Frank may have excluded the best of Latin American writing, but his choices had been readily approved by the prominent Latin American critics. For instance, Luis Alberto Sánchez would often vent his anger over those who eschewed regionalism of the kind Frank prized: "El caso de Borges, como el de [Oliverio] Girondo, es de impermeabilidad americana. A mí no me impresiona sino como europeo." [Borges, like Girondo, is impervious to America. They strike me as Europeans.][89]

Ironically, Frank's most lasting contribution to Latin American literature moved in a direction opposite to the prevailing Americanist one he had supported. In 1929 he had befriended Victoria Ocampo. With the help of Argentine novelist Eduardo Mallea, Frank persuaded Ocampo to start a literary magazine that would serve as a bridge between the two Americas. Ocampo traveled to New York in 1930 to discuss the format and editorial position of the forthcoming publication, later called *Sur*. In time it became the most prominent cultural review in South America, one that not only introduced Virginia Woolf and William Faulkner to Latin Americans, but also brought talented authors like Borges, fellow Argentine Julio Cortazar, and Chilean María Luisa Bombal to international attention.

Yet, for all the interest Frank managed to arouse in Ocampo and the energy he devoted to the project, *Sur* turned out to be quite remote from his Americanist design. He had envisioned a magazine that would publish nativist literature from the western hemisphere. He had even dreamed up the name *Nuestra América* for a publication he thought would appear in Spanish and English. Moreover, he hoped that Ocampo's Parisian tastes could be balanced by the staunch Americanist stance of Glüsberg, whom he recommended as editorial advisor. His calculations failed when "the princess of good taste"—as he called Ocampo—and the "dynamic immigrant Jew" Glüsberg were unable to reconcile their differences.[90] Ocampo, who financed the venture, remained with the journal and marked it with her distinctly cosmopolitan preferences. Frank, however, did not dissociate himself from the magazine. He remained an active contributor and member of the editorial board for over a decade. In spite of their opposing views in literature and politics, Frank and Ocampo maintained a friendship that lasted a lifetime. Ocampo may have disparaged Frank's socialism and his fascination with the myth of a vital, tellurian Latin American culture, but she certainly appreciated his sympathy for her personal intellectual and spiritual concerns—feminism and mysticism. Though at home Frank had opposed radical feminists' separatism, he accepted Ocampo's less extreme version. Not only did he applaud her struggle for women's rights in Argentina in the 1930s, but he openly admired her free soul. Both Frank and Ocampo agreed that feminism was part of a larger search for communal and self-fulfillment. This search and her Woolfian obsession with expressing inner vision through writing had stirred her mystical feelings. Her visit to Tagore's retreat in Santiniketan, India, confirmed for her that art could convey glimpses of the spiritual universe. Like Frank, Stieglitz, Eduardo Mallea, and in some ways Güiraldes, Ocampo thought the evocative symbols of art could recapture antirational conceptions of the world.[91] The secret of their affinity seems to have been tolerance and unrelenting honesty. Ocampo never hesitated to tell Frank that his Americanism was an impossible dream or that her predilections had always been closer to Europe. She would even address him in French: "Mon cerveau est en Europe et mon coeur en Amérique." [My mind is in Europe and my heart in America.][92] Ocampo also candidly rebuked his contention that Latin America had untapped spiritual and artistic potential. For her, the continent was hopelessly buried in poverty and apathy:

Waldo cher, qu'est-ce qui s'est passé avec la race espagnole? Panama et Pérou me consternent . . . comme nos provinces et l'Uruguay me consternent. . . . En fait pour vivre en Amérique du Sud vierge de consternations je m'aperçois qu'il me faut rester dans le tout petit cercle que je me suis fabriqué.

[Waldo dear, what has happened to the Spanish race? Panama and Peru shock me just as our provinces and Uruguay do. In fact, to live in South America free of shock I need to remain within the small circle that I have carved out for myself.][93]

Ocampo's refutation of Frank's ideas did not entail an outright dismissal of Americanism, but simply a redefinition. In her view, Americanism had original contributions to make to Western culture, to which she argued the two Americas belonged: "Para mí la América del Sur se halla aún a tal punto mezclada a Europa, empapada de Europa . . . que no es posible evocar a la una sin que la otra surja." [South America is so entangled with Europe, so soaked in Europe . . . that it is not possible to think of one without evoking the other.][94]

Ocampo was determined that *Sur* would take a more generous course that would promote both Frank's Americanism and Latin American writers who followed European modernism. The journal was to be a place where prominent European and North American intellectuals could mingle with local talents. No particular ideology underpinned Ocampo's editorial policy, just overt revulsion for those she thought did "not write well. I do not publish those people. . . . I never have, I never will."[95] The first issue of the magazine appeared in 1931. Its contents clearly reflected Ocampo's goals. She featured Frank's Americanist article "The Atlantic World," Walter Gropius's "The Whole Theater," and essays by Alfonso Reyes and Borges.

Later *Sur* devoted entire issues to the work of D. H. Lawrence and the latest in French literature. In 1944 Ocampo backed Frank's efforts to secure Argentina's support for the Allied cause and produced an issue focused on the United States. It gave Latin Americans a chance to read writers like Mary McCarthy, e. e. Cummings, Marianne Moore, and others hitherto unknown to them. The translation of the poems in the volume was left to Borges and Adolfo Bioy Casares, who produced outstanding versions. After the end of World War II, *Sur* continued to publish works by American authors and articles on American literature. For instance, in 1950 it ran two lengthy pieces on Poe; in 1957 Harriet de Onís discussed Eugene O'Neil for Latin American readers; and in 1958 the magazine carried an interview with Marianne Moore.

Frank often deplored the fact that Ocampo published too many "foreigners" and neglected authors from Peru, Colombia, and other South American countries. Ocampo disregarded his pleas and openly expressed her contempt for the regionalist fiction Latin Americans were writing in the thirties:

Entre nous ce qu'il y a dans ces pays, comme dans le notre est maigre, maigre, maigre à faire pitié. Croyez vous qu'il y ait des raisons pour respecter la mauvaise littérature hispanoaméricaine? Moi pas, je l'exècre. L'essentiel du *Sur* doit résider que jamais paraisse dans ces pages ce lourde galimantia que sont le fait de l'écrivain hispanoaméricaine.

[Between you and me, what there is in countries like ours is feeble, so feeble that it is pitiful. Do you believe that there are reasons to respect bad Latin American literature? I do not. I despise it. *Sur*'s stance is never to allow in its pages this heavy burden that constitutes the Latin American writer's achievement.][96]

The Latin American literature that remained closest to Ocampo's heart, and that provided the staple ingredient in *Sur*, was experimental. In 1939 the magazine published two stories by María Luisa Bombal:

"That Tree" and "The New Islands." In 1948 Cortázar's "The Death of Antonín Artaud" appeared; Uruguayan Juan Carlos Onetti's "The Album" was published in 1953. Of all Latin American writers, undoubtedly *Sur* favored Borges. He was a regular contributor to the journal and saw "Tlön, Uqbar, Orbis Tertius," "The Circular Ruins," and many other of his "fictions" first printed in its pages.

Ocampo's cosmopolitanism drew sharp criticism from the regionalists. Frank was caught in the midst of this strife. Luis Alberto Sánchez proved to be one of Ocampo's worst enemies. He accused her of destroying the Frankian spirit that had swept the hemisphere:

Victoria es mala americana. Eso es todo ... he aquí como Europa a veces nos da el método y otras veces nos quita el alma. Para los primero hay que llamarse Frank ... Güiraldes, Rivera, para lo segundo le recordaré Victoria, a Borges.

[Victoria is a bad Latin American. That's all ... this is how Europe sometimes gives us the method and others robs us of our soul. To be in the first category, one must be called Frank, Güiraldes, Rivera; as for the second, I'll remind you of Victoria and Borges.][97]

The Chilean poet Gabriela Mistral was equally critical of *Sur* 's editorial policy. Ocampo's biography of T. E. Lawrence published in 1942 triggered this note to Frank: "Nunca le perdonaré que no se atreva con una biografía de un criollo donde ponga cuanto sabe de la tierra." [I'll never forgive her for not daring to work on the biography of a Latin American where she can include all she knows about the soil.][98]

Samuel Glüsberg went so far as to propose forming an alliance of Americanist writers that would counteract the influence of *Sur*. It would include contributors to his publication *Vida Literaria* in Buenos Aires, as well as editors of *Indice* in Santiago de Chile, *Presente* in Lima, and *1930* in Havana.[99] The project never materialized, and it was Ocampo's definition of Americanism that triumphed. By being open to Europe and the United States, her magazine made possible the first steps toward the diffusion of Latin American authors outside the western hemisphere. *Sur*'s contacts with French writer Roger Caillois, who lived in Buenos Aires during World War II, enabled Latin American authors to be known in France, and after France in the United States. When Caillois returned to Paris in 1946 he translated Borges's *Ficciones* (1944). The book inaugurated the Editions Gallimard series La Croix du Sud, which published exclusively Latin American writing in translation. Later in the fifties and sixties. Caillois's project turned out to be a source of inspiration for American publishers.[100]

Though Frank refrained from attacking Ocampo, he never fully forgave her contempt for Americanist writing. In his *Memoirs* he confessed that she "overvalued, perhaps, her friends Tagore, Virginia Woolf . . . [and] the coteries of London and Paris. She undervalued surely some of the Americans; north and south, past and present: Brazil with such giant works as Euclides da Cunha's *Os Sertões* and her own pampa *Martín Fierro* meant little to her."[101]

Aside from Sánchez, Glüsberg, Mariátegui, and Ocampo, Frank carried on an active correspondence with Gabriela Mistral and Eduardo Mallea. Of the two, Mistral was a more devoted Americanist. Both her dedication to the cause of Latin American cultural unity and her pantheistic poetry suited Frank well. On her death in 1957, he wrote: "She came from the mineral mountains and deserts of Northern Chile. . . . She was very tall, and she walked more like an Indian than a European. . . . For if Gabriela made one think of her Andes in all their immobile composure . . . she was also the laureate of her vast American earth."[102]

Frank deplored American indifference to Mistral's poetry. Though her work had appeared in Catholic school texts, outside this context it was unknown. Alice Stone Blackwell had included some of Mistral's poems in her anthology *Some Spanish American Poets* (1938). Yet the collection failed to catch critical attention. For Frank, Mistral epitomized Latin American reverence for the arts. Her poetry was widely read in Latin America and her work as an educator highly respected. When she received the Nobel Prize in 1945, the Chilean government appointed her a lifetime consul. "A cultural world," Frank commented, "that loves and uses its poets in this fashion . . . has a health deeper than its political shortcomings."[103]

Mistral and Frank read each other's work avidly. The poet delighted in Frank's fiction. Remarks like this may have soothed the pain of his oblivion at home: "Novelas, Frank, no las deje usted, que eso es la semilla misma de su alma." [Frank, don't set aside your novels. They are the seed of your soul.][104]

When Mistral was teaching at Vassar in the forties, she tried to assist Frank in his efforts to make Latin American culture known in this country. She was convinced that in order to overcome indifference, it was necessary to find alternatives to anti-imperialistic rhetoric and address the American public in its own language, "dentro del espíritu de la

lengua inglesa, sin florituras." [within the spirit of the English language, without floweriness.][105]

Frank's fiction left a deep imprint on the work of Eduardo Mallea.
The novelist's ponderings about the nature of the self and national identity were akin to Frank's preoccupations. In 1934 Mallea collaborated
with writer María Rosa Oliver in the translation of Frank's *City Block*.
For Mallea, Frank became a spiritual and literary mentor: "I think a lot
about you while I'm writing. . . . You are in a way my confessor."[106]
Elsewhere, he admitted that he had written *Nocturno Europeo* (1935)
with the master in mind.[107] Despite his admiration of Mallea, Frank
never tried to have him published in this country. After 1945, Frank's
influence in Latin America lessened considerably. Only the old
generation of realists bothered to keep up their friendship with him.
Rómulo Gallegos, then president of Venezuela, commissioned Frank to
write a biography of Simón Bolívar, which Frank entitled *Birth of a
World: Bolívar in Terms of his People* (1951). Like the younger generation of writers in the 1960s, he became an enthusiastic admirer of the
Cuban revolution and published *Cuba: Prophetic Island* (1961). This
sympathetic account of Castro's socialist experiment elicited scant interest. More concerned with Joyce and Faulkner, the new generation had
lost all interest in regionalism and considered Frank's ideas obsolete.

Yet, with all its flaws, Frank's endeavor is important because he
broke the ice between the two literatures. Though reluctant to consider
anything that deviated from his Americanist ideology, he provided publishers with the first incentive to put out Latin American literature in
this country. In Latin America, he was more successful because he
managed to arouse interest in U.S. culture among important authors and
critics.

NOTES

1. For a study of the culture and intellectual debates of the early decades
of the twentieth century, see Edward Abrahams, *The Lyrical Left*
(Charlottesville: The University Press of Virginia, 1986); and Peter Conn,
The Divided Mind: Ideology and Imagination in América, 1898–1917
(Cambridge: Cambridge University Press, 1981).

2. For a discussion of Waldo Frank's interest in the Hispanic mind, see
Michael Ogorzaly, "Waldo Frank: Prophet of Hispanic Regeneration"
(unpublished Ph.D. dissertation, University of Chicago, 1982).

3. Probing coverage of American intellectuals' fascination and rejection of Europe before and after World War I can be found in Frederick Hoffman's *The 20's* (London: Collier Macmillan, 1965); Malcolm Cowley's *Exile's Return: A Literary Odyssey of the 1920's* (New York: Viking, 1951); and Malcolm Bradbury and David Palmer's *The American Novel and the 1920's* (London: Edward Arnold, 1971).

4. Abrahams, *Lyrical Left,* 2–3.

5. Quoted in Alfred Kazin's *On Native Grounds* (New York: Harcourt Brace Jovanovich, 1970), 172.

6. Romain Rolland, "America and the Arts," *The Seven Arts* 1 (November 1916), 47–8.

7. Waldo Frank, "Vicarious Fiction," *The Seven Arts* 1 (January 1917), 294.

8. Waldo Frank, "Emerging Greatness," *The Seven Arts* 1 (November 1916), 73.

9. See Abrahams, *Lyrical Left,* 85–91.

10. Peter Conn, *Divided Mind,* 316.

11. Waldo Frank, *Our America* (New York: Boni and Liveright, 1919), 96.

12. Juan José Tablada, "México en Norteamérica: cómo se juzga nuestra cultura," *Repertorio Americano* 3 (13 March 1922), 404–6.

13. Quoted in Arnold Chapman's "Waldo Frank in Spanish America: Between Journeys, 1924–1929," *Hispania* 47 (September 1964), 513.

14. Ibid., 14.

15. See Jerome W. Kloucek, "Waldo Frank: The Ground of his Mind and Art" (unpublished Ph.D. dissertation, Northwestern University, 1958), 417.

16. See Daniel Aaron, *Writers on the Left* (New York: Harcourt, Brace and World, 1961), 79.

17. Matthew Josephson, *Life Among the Surrealists* (New York: Holt, Rinehart, and Winston, 1962), 232.

18. Richard Pells, *Radical Visions and American Dreams: Culture and Social Thought in the Depression Years* (New York: Harper and Row, 1973), 22.

19. Maxwell Geismar, "Books and Things," *New York Herald Tribune,* 29 May 1948, 7.

20. Alfonso Reyes, "Introducción," *España virgen, escenas del drama espiritual de un gran pueblo* (Buenos Aires: Editorial Losada, 1947), 13.

21. Waldo Frank, *Memoirs of Waldo Frank,* ed. Alan Trachtenberg (Amherst: University of Massachusetts Press, 1973), 132–33.

22. Waldo Frank, *Virgin Spain* (New York: Boni and Liveright, 1926), 249.

23. Waldo Frank to Evelyn Scott, 5 September 1930, Harry Ransom Humanities Research Center, The University of Texas at Austin (hereafter, HRHRC, UT, Austin).

24. Frank, *Virgin Spain*, 72.

25. Sacheverell Sitwell, "Virgin Spain," *The Dial* 82 (January 1927), 65.

26. Federico de Onís, *Waldo Frank in América Hispana* (New York: Instituto de las Españas en Estados Unidos, 1930), 246.

27. Ernesto Montenegro, "Virgin Spain," *Literary Review of the New York Evening Post*, 20 March 1926, 2.

28. Waldo Frank, *América Hispana* (New York: Garden City, 1931), 265.

29. Hart Crane to his father, 20 May 1926, *Letters of Hart Crane and his Family*, ed. Thomas S. W. Lewis (New York: Columbia University Press, 1974), 493.

30. D. H. Lawrence, "America, Listen to Your Own," *New Republic*, 15 December 1920, 69.

31. Carleton Beals, *The Great Circle* (Philadelphia: J. B. Lippincott, 1940), 199–200.

32. Edward Weston, *Daybooks*, ed. Nancy Newhall (Rochester, N.Y.: George Eastman House, 1961), I, 190.

33. Hart Crane to Waldo Frank, *The Letters of Hart Crane, 1916–1932*, ed. Brian Weber (New York: Hermitage House, 1952), 372.

34. Frank, *Memoirs*, 157.

35. Ibid., 160.

36. M. J. Benardete, *Waldo Frank in América Hispana*, 7.

37. Waldo Frank, *Primer mensaje a la América Hispana* (Madrid: Revista de Occidente, 1930), 280.

38. Benardete, *Waldo Frank in América Hispana*, 231–32.

39. Victoria Ocampo to Waldo Frank, no date, Waldo Frank Collection. University of Pennsylvania Libraries (hereafter, WFC, UPL).

40. Juan José Sebreli, *Martínez Estrada: Una rebelión inútil.* (Buenos Aires: Editorial Palestra, 1960).

41. Frank, *América Hispana*, 185.

42. Sam Sloan to Waldo Frank, no date, WFC, UPL.

43. Waldo Frank to Evelyn Scott, 13 October 1932, HRHRC, UT, Austin.

44. Waldo Frank, "Contemporary Spanish America Literature," *Publishers Weekly*, 18 October 1930, 1842.

45. William Carlos Williams, *In the American Grain* (New York: New Directions, 1956), 229.

46. Frank, "Contemporary Spanish American Literature," 1842.

47. Waldo Frank, "The Hispano-American's World," *Nation*, 24 May 1941, 617.

48. José Eustasio Rivera to Waldo Frank, 19 June 1928, WFC, UPL.

49. Waldo Frank, "The Mexican Invasion," *New Republic*, 23 October 1929, 275–76.

50. Ibid., 276.

51. Waldo Frank, "Foreword," *Marcela: A Mexican Love Story* (New York: Farrar and Rinehart, 1932), x.

52. *New York Times*, 25 September 1932, 5.

53. Peggy Baird, "Marcela," *New Republic*, 14 December 1932, 143.

54. Chapman, "Waldo Frank in Spanish America," 520.

55. Waldo Frank, Typescript, no date, WFC, UPL.

56. Waldo Frank to Luis Alberto Sánchez, 21 February 1930, WFC, UPL.

57. John Farrar to Waldo Frank, 23 January 1930, WFC, UPL.

58. Samuel Glüsberg to Waldo Frank, 17 October 1928, WFC, UPL.

59. Roberto Payró to Samuel Glüsberg, 31 March 1928, WFC, UPL.

60. Jean Franco, *Introduction to Spanish-American Literature* (Cambridge: Cambridge University Press, 1969), 222.

61. Waldo Frank, "Foreword," *Tales from the Argentine* (New York: Farrar & Rinehart, 1930), x.

62. Margaret Wallace, "Vigor and Color in Tales from the Argentine Pampas," *New York Times Book Review*, 7 September 1930, 5.

63. Harriet de Onís, "Tales from the Argentine," *New York Evening Post*, 13 September 1930, 8.

64. John Farrar to Waldo Frank, 19 July 1930, WFC, UPL.

65. *Martín Fierro* quoted in Jean Franco, *Spanish American Literature*, 266.

66. Frank, *Tales*, xv.

67. See Sylvia Molloy, *La Diffusion de la Littérature Hispano-Américaine en France au XXè Siècle* (Paris: Presses Universitaires de France, 1972).

68. Adelina Güiraldes to Waldo Frank, 15 December 1932, WFC, UPL.

69. Ricardo Güiraldes, *Don Segundo Sombra: Shadows in the Pampas* (New York: Farrar and Rinehart, 1935).

70. John Farrar to Bullrich, 23 January 1930, WFC, UPL.

71. Federico de Onís to Waldo Frank, 1933, WFC, UPL.

72. Waldo Frank to Evelyn Scott, 8 September 1922, HRHRC, UT, Austin.

73. Waldo Frank to John Farrar, no date, WFC, UPL.

74. Waldo Frank to John Farrar, 3 April 1934, WFC, UPL.

75. Adelina Güiraldes to Waldo Frank, 13 July 1934, WFC, UPL.

76. Waldo Frank, "Introduction," *Don Segundo Sombra*, x.

77. Modern critics complain that Frank was romantically caught up with the mystique of Spain's purity and conveniently neglected the indigenous half of Latin America's origins.

78. Waldo Frank, "Introduction," *Don Segundo Sombra*, ix.

79. Anita Brenner, "Man's Fate in the Pampas," *Nation*, 30 January 1935, 133.

80. Fred T. Marsh, "A Tale of the Spanish-American Wild West," *New York Times Book Review*, 6 January 1935, 5.

81. "Gauchos of the Pampas," *Saturday Review of Literature*, 19 January 1935, 433.

82. Molloy, *La Diffusion*, 145.

83. Waldo Frank, *América Hispana*, 108.

84. Ibid.

85. John Farrar to Waldo Frank, 23 January 1930, WFC, UPL.

86. Percy Hutchison, "An Epic of the Argentine Pampa," *New York Times Book Review*, 16 August 1936, 6.

87. Molloy, *La Diffusion*, 204.

88. Waldo Frank, *South American Journey* (New York: Duell, Sloane, Pearce, 1943), 72.

89. Luis Alberto Sánchez to Waldo Frank, 30 June 1931, WFC, UPL.

90. Waldo Frank, *Memoirs*, 171.

91. See Doris Meyer, *Victoria Ocampo: Against the Wind and the Tide* (New York: George Braziller, 1979).

92. Victoria Ocampo to Waldo Frank, 22 January 1930, WFC, UPL.

93. Victoria Ocampo to Waldo Frank, 16 June 1930, WFC, UPL.

94. Victoria Ocampo, "Supremacía del alma y la sangre," *Testimonios*, serie 2 (Buenos Aires: Editorial Sur, 1941), 292.

95. See Mildred Adams, "First Lady," *New York Times Book Review*, 2 October 1966, 42.

96. Victoria Ocampo to Waldo Frank, 13 July 1931, WFC, UPL.

97. Luis Alberto Sánchez to Waldo Frank, 30 June 1931, WFC, UPL.

98. Gabriela Mistral to Waldo Frank, no date, WFC, UPL.

99. Samuel Glüsberg to Waldo Frank, 1 December 1930, WFC, UPL.

100. Molloy, *La Diffusion*, 207.

101. Frank, *Memoirs*, 165–66.

102. Waldo Frank, Typescript, 1 December 1957, WFC, UPL.

103. Ibid.

104. Gabriela Mistral to Waldo Frank, no date, WFC, UPL.

105. Gabriela Mistral to Waldo Frank, no date, WFC, UPL.

106. Eduardo Mallea to Waldo Frank, 1 May, no year, WFC, UPL.

107. For a discussion of Frank's influence on the work of Eduardo Mallea, see Arnold Chapman, *The Spanish American Reception of United States Fiction, 1920–1940* (Berkeley: University of California Press, 1966).

2

Blanche and Alfred Knopf's Literary Roundup

Blanche and Alfred A. Knopf were the most internationally minded publishers in New York during the twenties and thirties. Since 1915, when they established their publishing firm, the Knopfs had directed their attention to European writing, particularly Russian. In 1921 they made their first trip to Europe. In London they met Joseph Conrad, and in France they signed up André Gide. Soon after, they decided to balance their heavily European lists with a few Latin American titles. In 1922 they published Isaac Goldberg's study *Brazilian Literature*. In 1930 they issued *The Eagle and the Serpent* by Mexican novelist Marin Luis Guzmán.

Their interest in Latin America did not fully develop until the forties, however. Wartime conditions had closed off European travel and made necessary the exploration of new authors and markets for their list. Of the two Knopfs, Blanche was the most cosmopolitan. She spoke French fluently and some Spanish, felt at home in European literary circles, and had been personally involved in the firm's publication of Gide, Thomas Mann, and British writer Elizabeth Bowen. Thus it was only appropriate that she took advantage of the opportunity to travel in Latin America offered by Roosevelt's Good Neighbor Policy. In 1942 she set out on a literary scouting trip. This "literary roundup," as she later described her trip to Colombia, Chile, Peru, Argentina, Uruguay, and Brazil, gave her a chance to gain a firsthand view of what was being written, read, and published in Latin America.[1]

What struck her most was the fact that organized publishing in Latin America was all but nonexistent, with the exception of Argentina and, to a lesser degree, Brazil. In a continent where most writers relied on private publication and depended on government positions for a living, the visit by an American publisher immediately became a significant event. As Mrs. Knopf looked back on her stay in Peru, a single image seemed to stick in her mind: "Every time I opened my door [at her Lima hotel] there was a line of writers of varying kinds, essayists, poets etc., waiting the whole length of the corridor; no knowledge of what language we publish in, merely the fact that we publish [was] important to them."[2]

Far-reaching changes took place in Latin American literature during the forties. The realistic novel of social protest had lost its hegemony. More and more novelists were experimenting with new techniques and coming to terms with the fact that exploration of social questions did not require realism.[3] Although Mrs. Knopf cautiously regarded this trend as more indicative of "promise rather than achievement,"[4] the books she either contracted or deemed worthy of recognition reflected a desire to strike a balance between the traditional and the new. For instance, while in Peru she arranged to issue a selection of nineteenth-century author Ricardo Palma's "tradiciones." These short, zesty legends, set mainly in viceregal Lima reminded her of Washington Irving's *Sketch Book*.[5] In 1945 Palma's work appeared from Knopf as *Knights of the Cape*. Conversely, in Chile the publisher was impressed by María Luisa Bombal's innovative short novel, *The Shrouded Woman* (1938). With its use of stream of consciousness, Bombal's book had broken new ground in a way that made her work a landmark in Latin American fiction's advance toward modernity. Mrs. Knopf signed *The Shrouded Woman* in 1945. Having failed to realize that her contract with Knopf entailed surrendering her rights to supervise the translation, Bombal was surprised by the poor quality of the English version. She canceled the contract with Knopf and asked her friend Edmond Van Zweeland to buy out Knopf's first edition. The novel was published in 1948 by Farrar and Rinehart in the author's translation.

Argentina offered a wider spectrum of cultural achievement. Indeed, by 1940 Buenos Aires had replaced Barcelona as the center for Spanish-language publishing. There Mrs. Knopf came upon the existential work of Eduardo Mallea, who had already seen his *Fiesta in November* (1938) issued in the United States by Houghton Mifflin. Mrs. Knopf contracted Mallea's long novel, *The Bay Silence* (1940), which appeared in English in 1945. In retrospect, it seems puzzling that she chose Mallea as the representative Argentine author rather than Borges.[6] Mallea's local reputation and high visibility and Borges's more private personality may account for this oversight or preference. Perhaps the fact that

Borges did not write novels and had not yet achieved the stature he would with *Ficciones* (1956) also explains why his work did not appear as attractive to the publisher. In addition to Mallea, whose fame declined considerably after 1960, Mrs. Knopf met Victoria Ocampo. The editor of *Sur* was won over by Knopf's urbanity and shared her passion for French literature.

Brazil came last in Mrs. Knopf's tour, but it stood out in her mind for the vitality of its cultural scene. In Rio and Sao Paulo she met important publishers and booksellers who introduced her to the fiction of Jorge Amado. By then the novelist from Bahía was well known in Europe and the rest of South America. She signed Amado's *The Violent Land* (1940) and Graciliano Ramos's *Anguish* (1936), which were translated by Samuel Putnam and L. C. Kaplan respectively.

For a short time, the works Mrs. Knopf selected fed the officially promoted U.S. appetite for things Latin American, but soon after the war, public interest evaporated. Not so the Knopfs, whose allegiance to Latin American literature remained steadfast, despite an end to the "good neighbor" euphoria. With the reopening of Europe, audiences turned indifferent to Latin American writing and sought their foreign authors once again in the Old World. Part of the problem may have been that, lacking the necessary background, readers of South American works faced a particularly strenuous effort. As Brazilianist Samuel Putnam observed: "When Jorge Amado, for instance, describes a Negro Feiticeiro, or witch doctor, at his rites, we are likely to think that he is indulging in a bit of lurid melodrama; but anyone who knows his Brazil knows that this is not the case, for the sorcerer and the sorceress and such fetishistic ceremonies . . . are still of common occurrence."[7]

Finances posed another difficulty for the publishers. Although the Knopf archives do not reveal exact sales figures, correspondence abounds in complaints as to how poorly Latin American books fared. In a letter written in 1967 to Roger Stone, president of the Center for Inter-American Relations, Alfred Knopf maintained that his attachment to Brazil had proven to be quite costly: "Brazil has meant to me a great deal during the past quarter of a century. . . . I have involved my firm in substantial financial losses in trying to promote its literature."[8]

Apparently the greatest problem facing a publisher of Latin American literature was to find the right translators. Samuel Putnam's skillful renderings of Amado's *The Violent Land* and Gilberto Freyre's *The Masters and the Slaves* were rarities in a field characterized by mediocrity. When Putnam died in 1950, Harriet de Onís became the principal translator of Latin American books. Married to Federico de Onís, doyen of Spanish culture in the United States, she knew many of the authors personally and had traveled extensively in South America. When Mrs. de Onís became Knopf's chief translator, her reputation was already well established. She had brought into English Ciro Alegría's classic, *El mundo es ancho y ajeno* (1941). This novel, translated in the midst of "good neighbor" enthusiasm, won the Farrar and Rinehart Latin American fiction prize of 1941. Mrs. de Onís played a crucial role in Knopf's Latin American project, and until the mid-sixties, when new translators began to emerge, it was largely she who decided which novels would be translated into English. Notwithstanding the quibbles from certain reviewers—especially concerning her versions of Guimarães Rosa—Alfred Knopf relied heavily on her judgment and taste. He considered her "absolutely first rate," as he once declared to Jorge Amado.[9]

To some critics, Mrs. de Onís's translations belong to an earlier, less artistically sophisticated era of Latin American fiction. For them, her work seems to be indissolubly tied to the period of regionalism during the twenties and thirties. This assessment, however, seems misleading, for the works she translated were not restricted to purely realistic writing. Indeed, it should be noted that she either called to Knopf's attention or heartily praised such original and experimental works as Guimarães Rosa's *The Devil to Pay in the Backlands* (1956), as well as Alejo Carpentier's *The Lost Steps* (1953). Another important feature of Mrs. de Onís's contribution to Knopf's Latin American program was that she shared the publisher's penchant for Brazil. Like Alfred Knopf, however, she deplored the fact that every Brazilian writer counted on Knopf publication in the United States: "Every author thinks—if you want me to be charitable—hopes that his book is a masterpiece, if he can get it translated into English. That puts a five star cachet on it. Hence the flood of bad books we have to contend with. And probably most of your 'well meaning advisors and friends' and so on down the line haven't taken the trouble to read the books . . . [and] suggest that he/she send it to a publisher they know, which in the case of most Brazilians happens to be you."[10] But as she once confessed to editor Herbert Weinstock, she was "a softy where the Brazilians are concerned, a bit like Alfred."[11]

Ever since 1942, when Blanche Knopf had first visited Brazil, the country had held a special attraction to the publishers. Its appeal rested as much in Brazil's suggestion of a more diverse and hospitable environment than the rest of South America as in the fact that they made good friends among publishers and writers. Throughout the fifties and sixties the Knopfs continued to visit Brazil and to crusade for the diffusion of its culture in the United States. For these services the Brazilian government made Mrs. Knopf "cavaleiro" of the national order of the Southern Cross in 1950. In 1964 she was promoted to the rank of officer.

The Knopfs often lamented American lack of interest in things Brazilian. Alfred Knopf's main complaint was that rarely did the press "rush to review favorably or not [his] Brazilian books."[12] Despite his scant hopes that reviewers would mend their ways, Knopf regularly made them aware of this neglect. As he commented to Roger Stone, president of the Center for Inter-American Relations, in 1967: "I am hoping to take Sunday *New York Times* editor Max Frankel to lunch and do a little vigorous complaining. . . . Since this will be a repeat performance of a lunch I had with him and John Oakes a couple of years ago, I don't hope for much. . . . The *Times* is like Henry II: 'Never complain, never explain.' "[13]

After Blanche's death in 1966, Alfred kept up his Brazilian contacts. In 1967 he chose Rio as the site for his marriage to novelist Helen Norcross Hedrick. By the sixties he had also become something of an unofficial ambassador for matters concerning Brazil. He voiced his concern about the negative press given the Brazilian military regime and displeasure over the disregard for the importance of Brazil in hemispheric cultural affairs. In order to counteract what he deemed the misrepresentation of Brazil in the symposia organized in 1967 by the Inter-American Foundation for the Arts, he was quick to ask: "Aren't you inviting too many from Argentina . . .[?] Considering the mess the Argentines have made of their country I think their representation should be on the small side. Conversely, I think that you have far too few from Brazil . . . failure to invite at least Freyre would reflect on the foundation."[14] He justified this persistent lobbying for Brazil by stressing the increasing importance of Brazil in international affairs. A letter to Sir George Bolton, the chairman of the Bank of London and South America, attests to these feelings: "Brazil is worth to the United States, probably presently, but most assuredly in the long run as much as all the Spanish American countries put together."[15]

I

No other author can better represent the Knopfs' affection for Brazil than Jorge Amado. In 1970 he was the only South American who could boast of having seven titles published in English. Aside from being Brazilian, however, there were bound to be other reasons to account for Amado's publication record. To begin with, his work has proven to be relatively easy to translate; even with its generous use of the vernacular, Amado's prose is quite simple. Mrs. Onís would acknowledge this fact by maintaining that she had reached a point where she could "translate him without reading."[16] Elsewhere William Koshland confirmed her view: "It is clear that you do have the flair for doing Amado (even if your heart isn't in it)."[17] Furthermore, Amado was an entertaining storyteller, despite his weakness for overly entangled plots. His credentials were almost impeccable. By 1955 his writing had been translated into twenty-four different languages, including French, Spanish, and German. All of these aspects of Amado's work and career made him appear to be a low-risk author, one who could appeal to many different audiences. On the one hand, his novels were documents of an exotic, sensuous culture that fit the most popular image of Latin America, and on the other, some episodes of his work displayed craftsmanship that would permit his being considered more than a popular author or an exotic curiosity. As critic Jon Vincent observed, Amado's works are an "amalgam" of two inseparable elements. Though there is the Amado "who keeps foisting off historical or logical dates, there is also the 'poetic' Amado, but one can't set them apart."[18]

In general, Amado's work has a documentary, or overtly political, bent. At times, as Brazilian critics have often noted, the preeminence in Amado's writing of protest, rather than esthetic values, has been detrimental. In spite of this tendency, many of the novels issued by Knopf show that Amado is also capable of striking a balance; in fact, they all belong to what critic Fred Ellison calls his "second phase . . . initiated by *Jubiaba*, which reflects the author's new concern for literary technique and refinement of style."[19] *The Violent Land* also belongs to his "second phase," yet its polished craftsmanship and less politicizing did not make it less of a financial risk to publish in 1945, when the American literary scene was undergoing deep transformations. The war was over, and the mood had passed for documentary, or even slightly sociological, writing. More concerned with the self than with life in society, American authors of the forties had turned to the exploration of existential themes such as alienation and man's spiritual homelessness. In an attempt to describe the intellectual climate that permeated the fiction of authors like Bellow, McCullers, and Salinger—all three had published important works by the mid-forties—critic Ihab Hassan observed that "the world in our time seems to have either vanished or become a rigid, intractable mass . . . mediation between self and world appears no longer possible—there is only surrender and recoil."[20] Understandably, in an atmosphere charged with existentialism, an epic account of the struggle for Brazilian cocoa groves would be perceived as a holdover from the thirties.

In the *New York Times Book Review*, critic Nancy Flagg seemed overwhelmed both by the theme and style of *The Violent Land*. Disagreeing with arguments by Brazilianists like Ellison that the book avoided stereotypical characterizations and ideological outbursts, the reviewer deplored the work's lack of subtlety: "It isn't likely that this book has lost very much in translation. Too much is left, too much style for style's sake, too much indignation with the powerful and pity for the poor . . . too much love and lust and greed . . . and killing . . . the only deficit is humor."[21]

One of the few magazines to take notice of Amado's novel was the *New Yorker*, and it was even more critical, dismissing the work as interesting exotica: "The background is the wild, lush countryside of eastern Brazil when everybody was grabbing land amid a turmoil that makes the 'violent' of the title seem an understatement. . . . Interesting of its kind, but you may find it difficult to decide just what kind it is."[22]

Almost twenty years later, when Knopf issued a second Amado novel, the fortunes of the Bahian author took a dramatic turn. In fact, *Gabriela, Clove and Cinnamon* (1958) became the first Latin American best seller. Surprised by the financial and critical success of this lively novel, Knopf commented to Amado in 1963: "These earnings of yours [$9,683.96] are probably greater than any Latin American novelist has ever received from a North American publisher."[23] There was a great deal of excitement surrounding the American appearance of *Gabriela, Clove and Cinnamon* in 1962, and unlike other Latin American books, it was welcomed both in New York and throughout the country. Direct testimony of its popularity was the hearty recommendation it received from reviewers in the *Chicago Sunday Tribune*, the *San Francisco Chronicle*, and the *Springfield Republican*. The reasons for the appeal of *Gabriela* were many: it was humorous; it moved swiftly and contained an adequate supply of romantic plotting; and aside from its sociological implications, the novel read more like a tropical version of "Cinderella" than anything else. Also, the visual presentation of Juan de Onís's thorough review in the *New York Times Book Review* encouraged readers to see the work as an exotic romantic novel. Indeed, the insertion of a large portrait of an attractive mulatto woman holding fruit in her right hand not only reminds one of a Brazilian Tourist Office poster but also plays down the fact that *Gabriela* is largely about "Brazilian reality and change," about its transformation from "a patriarchal plantation society into a modern integrated, urban nation."[24] Knopf's good fortune in the choice of reviewers was instrumental in the novel's success. Juan de Onís, Harriet and Federico de Onís's son, not only shared their inclination for Latin America, but as the correspondent in Rio for the *New York Times* he had experienced firsthand the novel's popularity in Brazil. In four years it had sold over a quarter of a million copies, going through eighteen editions. Furthermore, Juan de Onís's lengthy review praised Amado's turning away from obvious political propaganda: "*Gabriela* represents undoubtedly the artistic liberation of Senhor Amado from a long period of ideological commitment to Communist orthodoxy.... In his earlier novels of the cacao region ... Senhor Amado tended to paint caricatures rather than characters: the girl from the backlands was either a prostitute or a Communist militant.... In striking contrast to these flat symbols, the characters in *Gabriela* are created in-the-round: they live, breathe and feel as genuine individuals."[25]

At the *Saturday Review*, *Gabriela* was assigned to Harriet de Onís, who, as would be expected, was no less enthusiastic: "One hardly knows what to admire most: the dexterity with which Amado can keep a dozen plots spinning; the gossamer texture of his writing; or his humor, tenderness and humanity."[26] Most of the other reviewers followed the example of the Onís family, differing only in length and in the inclusion of a positive note on the translation, which was also a key to its success. The smooth English version of *Gabriela* was not attained, however, without an effort. Disappointed with the rendering by James Taylor, Knopf had called in William Grossman to create a more polished product. Grossman, who had lived in Brazil and translated the work of Machado de Assis, produced what perhaps to this day is the best English version of an Amado novel. Unfortunately for Amado, his honeymoon with American readers ended with *Gabriela,* which wound up in Hollywood as a film. His next novel, *Home Is the Sailor* (1961), issued in the United States in 1964, did not fare as well. Amado's explicit politicizing impeded the acceptance of his next book as well—the short novellas contained in *Shepherds of the Night* (1966), which appeared in 1967. With the exception of one reviewer, who found in the novellas an affinity with Steinbeck's *Cannery Row* (1945),[27] the general trend was to dismiss the book in very harsh terms. John Duncan in the *New York Times Book Review* wryly lamented: "Amado's world is that of The People. A World in which everybody is poor, healthy and happy. It's the poor who really live. The rich are sick. . . . I must say that this mindless crowd bored me long before the end of the last novella."[28]

Alfred Knopf did not seem perturbed by this response, as indicated in his observation to Harriet de Onís, the book's translator: "I also agree that it is far from top drawer Amado and in consequence I intend to play it down . . . and not raise any expectation of a big sale."[29] Similarly, the fate of *The Two Deaths of Quincas Water-Yell* (1961) was less than a happy one.

The appearance of *Dona Flor and Her Two Husbands* (1966) rescued Amado's sinking reputation. Although Harriet de Onís felt cloyed by its overabundance of "whores and cathouses etc., etc.,"[30] the novel enjoyed quite a warm reception. In many ways it repeated the history of *Gabriela*, only in a lower key. With no political overtones to annoy readers and an abundance of sex and spicy humor to entertain them, the novel proved to be a profitable venture. At first, however, the book did not seem that promising. When Harriet de Onís began working on *Dona Flor*, she predicted that it would not be well received in the United States: "But with laying aside of his social philosophy, Amado has tended to become somewhat narcissistic; Bahía has become the measure of his work and it is a small world . . . perhaps Amado is not Flaubert."[31] Certainly this assessment was applicable to his other novels, but in the case of *Dona Flor* the subtle detachment with which Amado approaches his familiar territory outweighs his repetitiveness and his indulgence of local color. In the *New York Times Book Review* David Gallagher was quick to note this refreshing aspect of *Dona Flor*: "[It] is a remarkable novel for the coolness with which the author is able to impose his extraordinary characters on us. Like them we learn to take exoticism and magic in our stride."[32]

Amado's spell of good fortune, however, came to an abrupt end with the publication in 1975 of *Tereza Batista: Home from the Wars* (1972). The few reviewers who took notice of its appearance were particularly harsh in their criticism. In the *New Republic* William Kennedy did not

mince words: "Tereza Batista is a lithe and loving copper colored saint
. . . a prism of strength, a champion prostitute . . . a martyr to charity, a paradigm of virtue and fidelity . . . but also sad to say rather a
bore and a literary joke. . . . Amado believes not only in repeating
himself 4, 5, 6 times but also in summarizing each of Tereza's adventures so that we are not only drowned in verbosity but are also denied
the surprise that even rotten fiction can usually dangle before us."[33]
Thomas Lask's attack in the *New York Times* was a touch milder, but
when it lamented Amado's rehashing of an "old stock plot,"[34] this brief
comment aroused great anger in Knopf. He voiced his frustration by arguing that the *Times*'s treatment of the book was "insulting to the
most popular writer of the most important Latin American country. . . . I don't need to tell you [Roger Stone] that English is the
only language of thirty or so into which his books are translated where
they are so shabbily regarded."[35]

Even though Amado was praised in the United States for his storytelling abilities, his racy humor, and his occasional good characterization, he encountered a mistrust of his potential as a serious writer. As
Knopf observed to James Goodsell, the Latin American correspondent
for the *Christian Science Monitor,* "Sadly enough the critics who seem
to be on the saddle so far as Latin American letters are concerned . . .
view him with such contempt that his name is practically never mentioned. But still he is the only profitable writer of fiction among the
many Latin Americans we have published."[36] If in Brazil Amado had
partially overcome his reputation as a mere reporter on local color and
come to be appreciated as an important figure, in the United States, as
Knopf would grudgingly admit, it was quite a different story: "It is always difficult to have to put over a book by Amado. The reason is that
we have not with our best and most extravagant efforts succeeded in
making his name a household word."[37]

The story of Knopf's devotion to Brazil would not be complete without probing into his relationship with cultural historian Gilberto
Freyre. Freyre's view of Brazilian culture as the outcome of a unique
ethnic blend provided the necessary background for understanding the regionalist novelists Knopf had included in his publication lists. More
than that, Freyre's work had been the source for those writers and artists
like Amado, Ramos, and others who in the late twenties and thirties had
turned to the exploration of native themes and colloquial language.
Freyre's major work was *The Masters and the Slaves*, an interdisciplinary approach to Brazilian civilization in the vein of what some

American historians of the myth-and-symbol school would write in the fifties. First published in Brazil in 1933, Freyre's study was issued by Knopf in 1946 with an English translation by Samuel Putnam. The book had created a great stir in Brazil and to a lesser degree in Europe. In this country the author's reputable credentials—he had studied with Franz Boas at Columbia and taught at several major American universities—did not guarantee his acclaim. Although most reviews praised the impressive scope of the historian's undertaking, the first edition had little impact outside the field of Latin American studies. This changed, however, when the book was reprinted in 1956. In commenting on reaction to his book, Freyre always contrasted his French reception with that in the United States: "I am also inclined to think that European critics are considering my books from an angle that is not the same from which the same books are being considered by most American critics—as a rule specialists in Latin American subjects. For the Europeans (Febre . . . Gabriel Marcel . . .) my books are to be taken as something more than Latin American or Brazilian Studies. . . . European critics take my books as books that deal with particularities . . . of universal human problems."[38]

When it was made in the late fifties, Freyre's claim had some validity. Yet by 1963 and the English publication of *The Mansion and the Shanties* (1936), the sequel to his 1933 masterpiece, Freyre's work had reached a wider readership among American scholars. Not only was his interdisciplinary approach a more generally accepted methodology, but his views on slavery and miscegenation had been assimilated by historians concerned with the South and race relations in this country. Freyre, however, never ceased to view himself as an outcast from American intellectual circles. He grieved over the low estimation of his achievements and usually projected these feelings onto his American publishers. The focus for his dissatisfaction was often his translator, Harriet de Onís, who did not, he asserted, understand the implications of his scholarship. "She sees nothing in me besides a social historian," he told Knopf.[39] His accusations were often unfair, as Knopf himself admitted, for Freyre's discursiveness made the rendering of his work into English a burdensome task. Though acknowledging the seminal quality of his interpretation of Brazilian sociocultural development, Charles Wagley of Columbia also deplored the repetitiousness of Freyre's style and his tendency to "paint with a broad brush."[40] Similarly, Frank Tannenbaum of Columbia, Freyre's longtime friend and the author of the introductions to his two major works, judged the Brazilian's style to be an obstacle to full appreciation of his thought: "I know what a job it must have been to convert Gilberto's writing into readable English."[41]

When Barbara Shelby was assigned the translation of *Dona Sinha and the Father Son*, issued in 1967, Freyre seemed more satisfied and in a very uncharacteristic gesture expressed his approval of her performance: "The more I read the English translation the better I find it. Barbara is really what Brazilians describe now as Barbara: wonderful."[42] Freyre's relaxed attitude was quickly replaced by his usual petulance once reviewers rather condescendingly dismissed the book and his debut as a writer of fiction. John Wain in the *New York Review of Books* was representative of the critical reaction: "Freyre hasn't, it must be said bluntly, any idea of how to write a novel."[43] The Brazilian's dissatisfaction with his American reputation may have stemmed from a misperception of his status in this country. Used to being revered in his own land as an intellectual leader and a classic writer, Freyre expected to retain such a position when he came to the United States. It especially chagrined him to think that his status here was lower than that enjoyed by his fellow Brazilians. Even Knopf was forced to reassure his writer on this score: "I do not play favorites among my Brazilian authors. . . . I love you and while I have done my best to promote Amado and Guimarães Rosa as novelists, I have never referred to them in anything like the terms I habitually use when I speak of you."[44]

In many ways the story of Freyre's career is one of belated recognition. Bearing in mind, however, that he was presenting detailed studies of a relatively unknown culture to an audience that for the most part was more interested in Europe, the recognition he did receive was substantial. If Amado entered the scene at a time when social novels were out of fashion in this country, João Guimarães Rosa arrived at a more opportune moment. Unlike Amado, Rosa had broken with traditional regionalism and could compete on an equal footing with American novelists of the sixties. Like them, he favored fantasy rather than mimesis in fiction. His work also shared a comparable compulsion for playfulness in exploiting the disjunction between language and reality. And yet with all these marks of modernity and sophistication in his favor, Rosa found little but disappointment in his United States publishing fortunes. Although he was undoubtedly Knopf's most remarkable Brazilian author, he was also one whose publication involved the highest risks. Issued in English in 1963, Rosa had been brought to Knopf's attention by Harriet de Onís, who believed his craftsmanship to be in a class with that of Faulkner and Katherine Anne Porter. The translator had discovered one of Rosa's stories from *Sagarana* in an Argentine literary review and later translated "Duel" from the same collection for Noonday Press.[45] It is likely that Knopf was persuaded to take de Onís's advice when he learned that Rosa's *The Devil to Pay in the Backlands* had kept Brazilian critics amazed and bewildered ever since it first appeared.

Regarded as the local equivalent of *Ulysses*, few books had ever elicited so great a critical response in Brazil as *The Devil to Pay in the Backlands*. Ambiguous and at times haunting, the fiction of this doctor-diplomat was unprecedented in Brazilian literature. Not only had his work defied all traditional patterns, but it had literally revealed new possibilities for the Portuguese language. Furthermore, most critics have since acknowledged that Rosa's use of the Brazilian hinterland—the sertão—as backdrop avoided all constrictions of traditional regionalism and provided instead the setting for something dramatically new.[46] On a superficial level *The Devil to Pay in the Backlands* appears as a stream of consciousness version of a Brazilian western. Though a brief description of its plot—a gang leader's wanderings through the sertão in search of an evil murderer—does not suggest major difficulties, it is infinitely more complex. As professor of Brazilian literature and translator Gregory Rabassa warned its American publisher, "This guy is probably one of the hardest nuts to crack that has come along in a long time. The trouble is that he is good. I would put him next to Borges. Maybe even better in the long run."[47]

One of the many reasons for the difficulties involved in publishing such a novel is Rosa's stylistic distortions. In an attempt to elucidate this aspect of his work, critic Jon S. Vincent has written: "The narration [is] rendered in a gnomic style that combines the characteristics of a fanciful rural Brazilian speech and world view with some equally improbable elements of a likewise nonexistent erudite diction. . . . Among the high frequency forms found in [*The Devil to Pay in the Backlands*] are Latinisms, Indianisms, expletives, . . . and assorted morphological deformations."[48]

This list of Rosa's stylistic innovations naturally refers to the Portuguese version. If in the original language the novel had posed such enormous stumbling blocks to most readers, these difficulties multiplied when the work was brought into English in 1962 by translators Harriet de Onís and James Taylor. Looking back on the experience years later, de Onís commented to Herbert Weinstock: "I really find myself baffled by the work. . . . I recognize that the man has talent but I find it hard going. . . . I realize that it is a kind of poetry he is writing."[49]

When Rosa's novel was finally published in 1963, it was heeded by very few. One of the most perceptive appraisals came in the *New York Times Book Review* from William Grossman, who seemed to be drawn by the strangeness of its artifice. This attraction, however, did not prevent him from stating his misgivings about the translation: "The translators deserve our sympathy. How can one translate a book in which the substance is closely wed to a unique style. . . . In some passages even Brazilians find him hard to understand. The translators might have tried to devise an English style as close to that of Rosa's Portuguese as possible. The product would probably have been either brilliant or disastrous. They chose, instead, to employ a conventional style, with the result that much of the color is drained from the book."[50]

Always alert to new Latin American books, the *Saturday Review* ran an evaluation similar to Grossman's. Martin Price's assessment in the *Yale Review*, though less adulatory, welcomed Rosa's departure from conventional realism: "Its interest is more than documentary; the exotic setting is turned into a controlling symbol rather than picturesque background."[51] These positive reviews did not contribute, however, to a wider reception for the Brazilian's writing. Appealing only to a small group, the book existed in a kind of critical vacuum. Considered to be quite a revelation within the tradition of Latin American literature, even this caused difficulties for readers, since there were few precedents by which to judge it. Predictably then, Rosa's *Sagarana* (1946), a collection of nine stories, fared no better when it was issued in 1966, although Latin American fiction was beginning to be viewed in a new light. With novelist Carlos Fuentes of Mexico and Borges in the background, many critics seemed more prepared to accept narrative and linguistic innovations arriving from Latin America. Unfortunately, this gradual change in attitude did not alter the fate of the book. Realizing that Rosa required a larger circle of readers, Harriet de Onís suggested to Knopf's editor William Koshland that he should approach well-established American novelists who could endorse Rosa's work: "See that Bellow gets a copy [of *The Devil to Pay*]. He just might feel courageous to do a review by a runner-up for the Formentor Prize."[52] These hopes were apparently never realized, for the novel was reviewed only by the usual supporters of Brazilian fiction. In the *New York Times Book Review* Alexander Coleman dispelled any doubts about Rosa's modernity and assured the reader that he was being presented with a counterpart of Joyce: "Guimarães Rosa began the forging of a new language through prodigious linguistic play and the creation of new words. . . . [He] is a myth maker of the first order."[53] Once again William Grossman received Rosa with generous praise and seemed particularly amazed by the Brazilian's skillful insertion of the supernatural into everyday life.[54] Yet all these outbursts of enthusiasm were marred by disappointment over the quality of the translation. Notwithstanding the award bestowed on the translators of Rosa's novel, Mrs. Onís and James Taylor were the subject of critical disapproval, with both Coleman and Grossman maintaining that the translation had drained the vigor from the novelist's prose.

While *The Devil to Pay in the Backlands* had created numerous difficulties for its translators, *Sagarana* posed a double challenge:

The translator . . . dealing with any language but Portuguese is constrained to give a translation of a translation, because the text must be first rendered into a standard Portuguese in order to sort out meaning, before the transference is feasible. . . . In the case of English, the translator is faced with the task of "translating" from an artificial language which takes full advantage from [sic] the inflective character of Portuguese into a language which tends to alter meaning largely through the distribution of words rather than the addition of suffixes.[55]

Most Brazilianists would agree that the translation was the cause behind the limited appeal of Rosa's work. Indeed, what Harriet de Onís described as "the enormous stress and tension" to which the novelist submits his words makes his work unintelligible even for Brazilians.[56]

These difficulties, however, did not hinder Knopf from giving Rosa another chance. Discouraged by the outcome of her efforts with Rosa, Harriet de Onís refused to do "another book of his . . . because it's too exhausting," which forced Knopf to look elsewhere for a translator.[57] This turned out for the better, since Barbara Shelby felt more at ease with Rosa's writing. Not only did she have easier access to the author—she was an American diplomat stationed in Rio—but her ear for the subtleties of his language seemed to be infinitely finer. In her introduction to *The Third Bank of the River: Other Stories*, issued by Knopf in 1968, Shelby admitted that her endeavor had been "uncommonly difficult." Certainly this was a euphemism, as further comments made in a letter to Knopf clearly reveal: "Rosa claims . . . that my approach to the stories was philosophically right and that he saw no need to read the translation. . . . I fear that only a poet philologist, someone like Tolkien could do full justice to his poetic, somewhat precious style, which is beautiful but essentially untranslatable."[58]

When the book was issued, most critics agreed that these stories marked a change of direction in Rosa's fiction. Alexander Coleman wrote in the *New York Times*: "There is a difference: this is a book ... by a dying man. Guimarães Rosa suffered a near fatal heart attack in 1958. He emerged from this encounter another man and another writer ... the stories are much closer to the self, so much more essential."[59] Rosa's language had changed and become sparser and more subdued. This new phase did not necessarily mean that the translation difficulties subsided for Shelby, for the relative simplicity of language was accompanied by dense ambiguity. At times unsettled by the book's pervasive duplicity, Shelby would observe: "His preoccupation is entirely with the romance, music and poetry of the style, not with the meaning, and his advice is generally: Leave it a little vague."[60] Elsewhere she confessed to Knopf that Rosa's charming disposition was of little help: "Discouragingly often, he himself has forgotten why he invented such and such a word and what he intended it to mean."[61]

The Third Bank of the River appeared shortly after Rosa's death in 1967, and in an effort to make the book appear more familiar to English language readers, Shelby stressed in her introduction how close Rosa's work was to that of many American masters. In his use of the supernatural in everyday experience, he reminded her of Poe; his "transcendental seriousness" and extravagant language had affinities with Melville; and in his attachment to the land he echoed Faulkner.[62]

And yet with all these links to classic American literature, Rosa's collection achieved only a modest appreciation. Although Alexander Coleman and the reviewer in the *Saturday Review* recognized in Rosa another master and commended Shelby's careful translation, none of this significantly changed the Brazilian's fortunes, as he remained largely unknown to American readers. Appraising the general response to Rosa's work, Knopf was naturally dismayed: "Critics have been so disgusting up here in withholding any credit either to us or translators of three books of his which we have done that I am surely tempted to say the hell with it."[63]

Next to Rosa's work, Brazilian critics were most impressed by the fiction of Clarice Lispector. In this country, however, to compare the two in any way seemed unusually foreboding. After Rosa's reception, taking up a deeply introspective and equally hermetic novel did not seem a particularly enticing adventure. Thus Knopf turned down Lispector's *The Apple in the Dark* (1961) when it was first brought to his attention in 1963. With the exception of Harriet de Onís, who thought

Lispector's style was "extraordinary," readers assigned to evaluate the book were either disappointed or clearly antagonized. Knopf editor W. Trask, for instance, dismissed it as derivative: "The book seems a desperate attempt to imitate the avant-garde French novel. But whereas the French neglect their readers in their intense preoccupation with theme, Lispector approaches the method from the outside, conceives it as an endless series of games of 'Look you can't catch me' with a reader whom she deliberately blindfolds. . . . When she has time for Paris to wear off . . . she should be worth watching."[64]

Lispector, however, did not have to wait for the influence of the "nouvelle vague" to wear off, for with French publication she was given a second chance in America. It was not that Knopf's feelings had radically changed; he still believed that the novel was "an enormously difficult one for the reader and we will have the devil's time finding an audience for it."[65] Originally Knopf had intended to launch *The Apple in the Dark* with a translation by Elizabeth Bishop, which he believed would attract a wider readership, since aside from her established American reputation, she had lived in Brazil for fifteen years and was well read in Latin American literature. When these plans fell through, he turned to Gregory Rabassa, who knew the author personally and had discovered her for American readers with his translation of the story "The Crime of the Mathematics Professor," published by *Odyssey Review* in 1961. The choice of Rabassa could not have been better, for he proved to be one of the few translators prepared to respond to the extraordinary sense of language that permeates modern Latin American fiction. Rabassa's attitude is revealed in a letter to Knopf editor Herbert Weinstock: "I worry a lot about the genteel translations we get of gutsy Latin American stuff."[66] Rabassa worked on the novel while he was in Rio with a Fulbright-Hays grant in 1965. He had just finished Julio Cortazar's *Rayuela*, an extremely difficult task, considering that novelist's inventiveness and sometimes stubborn defiance of convention. In Lispector's *The Apple in the Dark* the translator found a more intricate undertaking than even he had anticipated: "I must say that most of the time I found it much more difficult to render than *Rayuela* and at times when I'm tired and I look at some other Brazilian book written in simpler prose, I say to myself, I wish I were translating that. On the other hand . . . this slow word for word reading of the book brings out all sort of things. . . . I was impressed with the book when I first read it and now I am twice as impressed."[67]

The most obvious obstacle posed by Lispector's work came from her disavowal of conventional syntactical structures, which Rabassa thought to be the essence of her fictional world. He commented that she marshals the syntax "in a new way that is closer perhaps to original thought patterns than the language had ever managed to approach before."[68] In his admiration for Lispector's novel, however, Rabassa stood alone. Knopf and Weinstock not only had faint hopes for its success but were ambivalent about its value. As Weinstock confessed to Rabassa: "I must tell you that I do not at all like the book—in fact rather dislike it. . . . Reading the book requires enormous patience and for me at least the result is not worth the great effort of concentration required."[69]

When the book was issued in 1967, Knopf's predictions were fulfilled. Few publications noticed its appearance, and those that did disagreed on its quality. In the *New York Times* C. D. B. Bryan pointed to the author's lack of control: "Her overwriting flaws the novel, especially where she waxes lyrical about intellectual and emotional minutiae."[70] Conversely, in the *Saturday Review* R. F. Goldman thought that the novel brought together themes common to most contemporary fiction: "The book is about many things: The relation between speech and act; knowledge and being; perception and awareness, reality and imitation."[71] Like Rabassa, Goldman thought that the novelist came close to Virginia Woolf in her poetic depiction of intimate thoughts and feelings. After reading his perceptive analysis, one senses that Lispector's poor showing was not due so much to the essential complexity of her novel but more to the fact that she did not quite fit the stereotype of a Latin American writer. Though she shared similar concerns with contemporary American writers, which should have assured a wider acceptance, her work was quickly dismissed.

One also senses that when it came to publishing Spanish American novelists, Knopf resorted to stricter selection guidelines than with Brazilians. He was less willing to rely on local reputations or a friend's recommendations. In the case of the Cuban Alejo Carpentier, Knopf was impressed by the author's European endorsement: Carpentier's novel *The Lost Steps* (1953) had been awarded the Prix du Meilleur Livre Étranger by Parisian critics in 1955. After ten years almost fully devoted to Brazilian regionalism, the inclusion of Carpentier in 1956 had added a new dimension to the Knopf Latin American list. Unlike Amado's earthy, somewhat provincial vision, Carpentier's experience of Latin America had a grandiose scope and probed deeply into the mysteries of time and history. A Cuban of French descent, Carpentier spent his youth in Paris, where he had met the surrealists and absorbed their obsession with the *merveilleux*. But as critic Jean Franco observes, "He was to find their imagination poor compared to the reality of the Caribbean. After a visit to Haiti in 1943 he discovered 'lo real maravilloso' ['marvelous reality'—a form of what García Márquez later referred to as 'magic realism'] at his own doorstep."[72] Carpentier's European credentials, which also included recognition in Britain, made American publication an even more promising venture. Seldom very enthusiastic about Latin American novels, editor Herbert Weinstock felt that they had something special in their hands: "It is not only one of the two or three novels ever to emerge from Latin America, but also a genuine work of art fiction."[73] Yet in trying to find an audience for the novel— an allusive tale of a composer who leaves New York for an ideal jungle community—Weinstock discovered that his impression was not widely shared. For readers of Faulkner, Carpentier's expansive prose ought not to have posed a barrier. Neither should his concern with withdrawal from civilization have sounded too esoteric, bearing in mind the works of Melville, Twain, and Hemingway. Yet these same characteristics were not reassuring enough for those asked to evaluate the novel. The baroque quality of his prose—overwrought with biblical, mythical, and classical allusions—proved to be quite unsettling to readers. Diana Trilling politely turned down an offer to write a statement on the book. But it was William Styron who seemed most puzzled. Though later he was to become quite receptive to Latin American fiction, in this instance he felt at sea; he simply did not know into what tradition to place the work: "I liked it in a strange way. . . . I found it so overpoweringly exotic . . . that in the end I just don't know what my opinion is. I read it much as if I were tasting some new tropical fruit whose flavor was quite unique and wonderful but which I had to turn down for the good old standby orange. . . . Too offbeat for my taste in fiction."[74]

If Styron had resorted to the standard label of "exotic" to dismiss it, Ralph Ellison was quite awed by *The Lost Steps*. He found a kindred spirit in Carpentier. The Cuban's delving into what is indigenously Latin American, and at the same time archetypal, seemed very appealing to someone so deeply concerned with the universality of Black experience: "I found it especially attractive that its hero is obsessed by those resonant questions which the Sphinx always puts to the hero when old certainties are shattered. . . . Not a little of my pleasure came because Carpentier's hero plunges back into those pre-literate cultures which are so often rejected because mistakenly regarded as primitive. . . . Carpentier knows that the trick for the sophisticated artist lies in learning once more to approach our own materials."[75]

When the book came out, most of the reviews were favorable. Reviewers in the *New Yorker* and the *Saturday Review* were equally impressed by the evocative power of Carpentier's prose. The critic in the *Yale Review* went so far as to pair the Cuban's name with Balzac's: "Because of the anthropological character of a good deal of the materials of *The Lost Steps* I think particularly of Balzac's *La Peau de Chagrin* (1837), where at the beginning of the story a vision is invoked of the success of epochs of human life and culture out of chaotic dusts of a museum."[76]

For his publishers, however, this unusual backing from reviewers was not regarded as significant. It would seem that for them only a stamp of approval from the *New York Times* meant real recognition for an author, and in the case of *The Lost Steps*, Selden Rodman, its reviewer, did not follow the trend set by other critics. Though impressed with Carpentier's style, Rodman avowed his mistrust of what he deemed an excessive display of erudition: "A story by and about an intellectual is not likely to be well received in America. . . . And despite my awareness of this national limitation—I find myself becoming not a little suspicious too when I find the protagonist discussing his sexual prowess in terms of the Greeks and the Israelites, invoking Descartes in a dugout canoe."[77]

However, it was the critic's discarding of the novel as "cheap" that unleashed the anger of Herbert Weinstock. In a letter to the editor he bitterly complained about the "unserious" nature of Rodman's words and pointed to what he considered to be an erratic and incongruous assessment of the novel. He thought it outrageous for Rodman to think that the novel was "cheap" after having maintained that it was "absorbing" and "erudite." The controversy was swiftly shelved when Rodman refused to address the charges of inconsistency and added that Carpentier's European credentials did not really impress him.[78]

Despite all the enthusiasm involved in the publishing of *The Lost Steps*, the book proved to be a commercial failure. Disregarding the perceptive critical recognition the book had received, Weinstock viewed the whole undertaking as flawed and as evidence of the anti-intellectual bias of most American readers. To stress this point he drew a parallel with Faulkner's reception: "Faulkner's complicated style—and particularly his almost endless sentences and paragraphs—long militated against his being accepted here."[79] Though the book made a poor financial showing, Weinstock had been sufficiently impressed by Carpentier to suggest a reissue of *The Lost Steps* in 1966. This time he believed that Carpentier's international stature should be played up and asked literary figures as diverse as Graham Greene and Carlos Fuentes for endorsement. Though he did obtain a blurb from Greene, Fuentes declined the offer to write an introduction. Notwithstanding his admiration for the Cuban, Fuentes asserted that Carpentier's uncritical pro-Castro standing had forced him to reconsider his previous commitment. The book was finally prefaced by British critic J. B. Priestley, who had written a commendatory review in the *Sunday Times* when the book was issued in London in 1956. Unfortunately, all this attention did not result in a better financial performance; the reprint sold less than 3,000 copies.

Carpentier's next novel, *The Pursuit* (1956), was turned down by Knopf. Its fragmented narrative and myriad political references were considered to be too dense to interest American readers. As Weinstock tried to explain to a surprised Carpentier, who believed political terrorism in Cuba in 1957 to be a familiar issue to most Americans, "It doesn't have for readers in this country enough signposts to prevent him from feeling that he is simply baffled."[80] It is puzzling to see that *The Pursuit* was rejected with the same arguments used to justify Knopf's 1957 publication of Carpentier's *The Kingdom of This World* (1949). Whereas the political allusions of *The Pursuit* were considered far too incomprehensible, those in *The Kingdom of This World*, presented in a less disjointed narrative form, seemed worthy of exploiting. Indeed, the publication of the story of a Haitian slave rebellion during the French colonial period appeared to be opportune because political unrest in that country was front-page material for the American press of the late fifties. As elaborate in its conception as *The Lost Steps*, the Haitian novel succeeded on a relatively larger scale than had the earlier work. In the *New York Times*, Mildred Adams drew on the currency of its plot and praised its skillful construction. The *Yale Review* and the *Atlantic Monthly* commended the non-naturalistic handling of the plot, one that would have been prime material for Carpentier's heavy-handed regionalistic predecessors.[81] For all the acclaim accorded *The Kingdom of This World*, it was not until 1970, when Knopf published *The War on Time,* that Carpentier won a wider circle of readers. Though less celebrated than García Márquez or Fuentes, his reputation has certainly benefited from the closer attention now paid to Latin American fiction.

Among Latin Americans, Chilean José Donoso was the most familiar with all the machinations of the American literary scene. A protégé
of novelist Carlos Fuentes, Donoso was introduced to Knopf in 1965
by the Mexican's literary agent Carl Brandt. Educated at Princeton and
winner of the 1962 William Faulkner Foundation Prize for his novel
Coronation (1957), Donoso must have seemed particularly appealing
because of the special aura of his work's cosmopolitanism. Unlike Carpentier's and Rosa's settings, Donoso's portrayal of decaying Chilean
aristocrats did not seem quite so remote. Though no less innovative in
his handling of his themes of isolation, tension between social classes,
and decomposition of the bourgeoisie, Donoso appeared to be more
universal, more intelligible for an urban reader. As Knopf editor Angus
Cameron described Donoso's work, it coincided with the modern world:
"He seems to be able to combine the outlook and style of two important traditions: Latin American and one that might be called European-
U.S. tradition."[82] The recognition of his international outlook did not,
however, prevent Donoso's American career from experiencing a sluggish start, inaugurated with the issuing of *Coronation* in 1965. Perhaps
it was his constant and obsessive desire to overcome the difficulties inherent in gaining a U.S. readership for a Latin American novel that
made the publication of Donoso's work often a strenuous task for his
publishers. Though the prize-winning novel was something of a classic
in Chile and the rest of South America, here it did not leave much of an
impression on its readers. Alexander Coleman's references to Donoso's
"bent for the macabre"[83] and Muriel Spark's description of it as a *me-
mento mori* did nothing to lessen the book's being what Cameron described as a "publishing loss."[84]

When Knopf decided to bring out *This Sunday* in 1970, Donoso was
teaching at the University of Iowa Writers Workshop. In the hope of
achieving a better reception for the book, Donoso followed the publication of his novel very closely. He himself selected his former student
Lorraine Freeman as his translator and supervised every step of her
work. Only Gilberto Freyre was so compulsive about his reputation.
From the moment Cameron read the manuscript of *This Sunday* he au-
gured that it would "not work commercially," that its ambiguity and
fragmented narrative "will only appeal to a very special audience."[85]
Donoso staunchly resisted any suggestions for stylistic changes. Assert-
ing that "even your Faulkner has been doing it for ages," he saw no reason for his editor's skepticism.[86]

Determined to gain a wider reading for the book, Donoso attempted to interest reviewers beyond the usual circle of critics of Latin American fiction. His targets were the established American novelists, with whom Donoso thought he shared similar technical and thematic concerns. He tried to obtain Katherine Anne Porter's endorsement, assuming her penchant for Latin America would help him: "She is under the impression that she invented Latin America . . . she might do something handsome."[87] As it turned out, Ms. Porter proved to be quite elusive and was never to read the book. Likewise, John Barth "quite plainly," as Donoso discovered, refused to write a blurb.[88] The pursuit of Saul Bellow, however, became his main obsession. Initially hopeful that he would receive a hearing from him, Donoso wrote to Cameron that "Saul Bellow was in town the day before yesterday and though I talked with him no more than five minutes he is reported to have taken a shine to me and wants to read my stuff."[89] As time slipped by and Bellow's silence became more ominous, Donoso would anxiously ask his editor: "If only Bellow . . . but will he?"[90] However, Bellow's elusiveness was offset by the interest taken in the Chilean's work by Kurt Vonnegut, who had befriended the author at Iowa. Vonnegut's endorsement could not have been more flattering to an author who envisioned himself—and rightly so—as part of the mainstream and resented any association with Amado or any other conventional Latin American novelist. To show that *This Sunday* transcended "Latin Americanism," Vonnegut delivered a blurb that was unusual in the deliberateness of its point: "It is a masterpiece—kaleidoscopic, beautiful, gentle, and mad. The English translation contains some of the most intricate games with language and point of view I have ever been dazzled by, *Finnegans Wake* excluded. . . . It would be perfectly fair to present Donoso as an American writer. . . . Donoso speaks English better than I do. He is an elegant product of Princeton with straw on his hair and dung on his shoes from two years of teaching at Iowa. This is a Chilean?"[91] Following in Vonnegut's steps, Alexander Coleman in the *New York Times* attempted to bank on Donoso's sophistication and international flair by unveiling the "faintly Jamesian" touch of his vision. The review pleased the author and the editor, but it did not win wider recognition. Observing how sophistication had not made a significant difference, Knopf lamented that he had published him "ten years too early."[92]

Benefiting from the aftermath of the "boom" in Latin American fiction, which had made many of its authors international stars, Donoso's

The Obscene Bird of Night (1970) won the acclaim he had longed for
when Knopf issued it in 1973. This long, intricate novel—wrought
with monsters and metaphors of decrepitude—had been painfully conceived and was seen by Donoso as the highlight of his career. In the
United States it was given a "modern masterpiece" stature by Robert
Coover's ecstatic celebration of it on the front page of the *New York
Times Book Review*. Coover was exuberant in his descriptions of
Donoso's "cabalistic design" and the power of his temporal and spatial
disarrangement.[93] What had begun with Donoso scrambling for the
support of an important figure had ended with his admission to the inner circle. Donoso's obsession with endless mutations, decay, and unre-
ality had made him a fellow traveler with Hawkes, Barthelme, and
Coover, as a reviewer argued in the *New York Review of Books*.[94]

Donoso's work continued to receive significant critical attention in
the late 1980s and early 1990s. *Curfew* (1986) and *Taratuta and Still
Life with Pipe* (1993) have not only come a good distance from the
phantasmagoric world of *The Obscene Bird*, but they have also proven
the characteristic versatility of his narrative discourse.

In tracing the careers of the Knopf Latin American authors, one dis-
covers two revealing, yet contradictory, views. On the one hand, there
is the picture of two solitary advocates of a remote, forgotten literature.
This image bears some truth, especially at the beginning of the undertaking when the Knopfs had to convince many North Americans that
there was worthwhile fiction being written south of their border. Yet
there is also an ambivalence at the center of the Knopfs' pioneering efforts. Unsure of the real value of some of the fiction that critics in
Latin America hailed as original and innovative, Alfred Knopf would often comment:

It is perfectly hopeless for us to take on Latin American authors simply on
the ground that they are either respectable, moderately good deserving [*sic*]
translation, unless they are so good or tell such a widely appealing story
that we could hope to have reasonable hope of getting a hearing from them.
My own opinion is that very few such writers exist especially in Latin
America though I know that every time I go to a party where many Latin
Americans are I come away with the feeling that there are at least two dozen
immortal masterpieces lurking all over the continent and only waiting for a
reasonably intelligent publisher to get them the hearing they deserve.[95]

At times Knopf even sensed that readers would be grateful to him if
he refrained from publishing such exotic writers: "I suspect were I to re-

tire from all publishing activities my colleagues would heave a great sigh of relief and say 'Now at any rate we're rid of the Latin Americans.' "[96] If ambivalence and occasional symptoms of condescension toward a literature that had proved quite difficult to market accounts for the skepticism with which the Knopfs undertook the publication of Rosa, Lispector, and even Donoso, it was their capacity to overcome these feelings that has left its mark on the American literary scene. Despite all their misgivings, the Knopfs provided a hearing for authors who at the time would have surely been dismissed by other publishers. However idiosyncratic their criteria for selection may now appear, it is only in the light of the present recognition awarded to Latin American literature that we can understand and fully appreciate the significance of their untiring efforts.

NOTES

1. Blanche Knopf, "The Literary Roundup: An American Publisher Tours South America," *Saturday Review of Literature*, 10 April 1943, 7–10, 34.

2. Blanche Knopf, "South America—1942," Typescript, 1942.

3. See Jean Franco, *Introduction to Spanish American Literature* and Emir Rodríguez Monegal, *El boom de la novela latinoamericana* (Caracas: Editorial Tiempo Nuevo, 1971).

4. Blanche Knopf, "The Literary Roundup," 7.

5. Ibid., 8.

6. Ibid., 9.

7. Samuel Putnam, *Marvelous Journey: A Survey of Four Centuries of Brazilian Writing* (New York: Alfred A. Knopf, 1948), ix.

8. Alfred Knopf to Roger Stone, 24 September 1975. All quoted correspondence in this chapter is from the Knopf Collection in the Harry Ransom Humanities Research Center, The University of Texas at Austin.

9. Alfred Knopf to Jorge Amado, 4 November 1964.

10. Harriet de Onís to William Koshland [Knopf editor], 8 July 1967.

11. Harriet de Onís to Herbert Weinstock, 6 March 1966.

12. Alfred Knopf to Mrs. H. Reid Bird, 1 October 1970.

13. Alfred Knopf to Roger Stone, September 1975.

14. Alfred Knopf to Robert Wool, 28 August 1967.

15. Alfred Knopf to Sir George Bolton, 22 May 1969.

16. Harriet de Onís to Alfred Knopf, 14 December 1967.

17. William Koshland to Harriet de Onís, 21 June 1967.

18. Jon S. Vincent, "Jorge Amado, Jorge Desprezado," *Luso-Brazilian Review* 15 (summer 1978), 14.

19. Fred P. Ellison, *Brazil's New Novel: Four Northeastern Masters* (Berkeley: University of California Press, 1954), 86.

20. Ihab Hassan, *Radical Innocence: The Contemporary American Novel* (Princeton, N.J.: Princeton University Press, 1961), 327.

21. Nancy Flagg, "The Violent Land," *New York Times Book Review,* 24 June 1945, 8.

22. "Briefly Noted: Fiction," the *New Yorker,* 23 June 1945, 69.

23. Alfred Knopf to Jorge Amado, 16 July 1963.

24. Juan de Onís, "The Town's Story Is the Land's," *New York Times Book Review,* 16 September 1962, 1.

25. Ibid.

26. Harriet de Onís, "Nacib's Fair Lady," *Saturday Review of Literature,* 15 September 1962, 96.

27. Sandra Schmidt, "Voodoo Acres," *Newsweek,* 30 January 1967, 94–95.

28. John Duncan, "The World of the People," *New York Times Book Review,* 22 January 1967, 4 and 38.

29. Alfred Knopf to Harriet de Onís, 27 June 1966.

30. Harriet de Onís to Herbert Weinstock, 15 February 1966.

31. Ibid., 19 August 1966.

32. David Gallagher, "Dona Flor and Her Two Husbands," *New York Times Book Review,* 17 August 1969, 3.

33. William Kennedy, *"Tereza Batista: Home from the Wars* by Jorge Amado," *New Republic,* 28 June 1975, 26–27.

34. Thomas Lask, "Tereza Batista," *New York Times Book Review,* 21 September 1975, 38.

35. Alfred Knopf to Roger Stone, 24 September 1975.

36. Alfred Knopf to James Goodsell, 5 January 1970.

37. Alfred Knopf to Barbara Shelby, 14 September 1970.

38. Gilberto Freyre to Alfred Knopf, 4 November 1959.

39. Ibid., 26 January 1962.

40. Charles Wagley, "Meet the Brazilians," *New York Times Book Review,* 12 May 1963, 3.

41. Frank Tannenbaum to Alfred Knopf, 5 June 1962.

42. Gilberto Freyre quoted by Alfred Knopf in a letter to Barbara Shelby, 1 June 1967.

43. John Wain, "Versions of the Pastoral," *New York Review of Books,* 4 May 1967, 36.

44. Alfred Knopf to Gilberto Freyre, 10 April 1963.

45. Harriet de Onís, "Translator's Note," *Sagarana* (New York: Alfred A. Knopf, 1966), xvi.

46. Wilson Martins, "Structural Perspectivism in Guimarães Rosa," *The Brazilian Novel* (Bloomington: Indiana University Press, 1976).

47. Gregory Rabassa to Herbert Weinstock, 16 March 1965.

48. Jon S. Vincent, *João Guimarães Rosa* (Boston: Twayne, 1978), 69.

49. Harriet de Onís to Herbert Weinstock, 10 November 1967.

50. William Grossman, "Outlaw with a Problem," *New York Times Book Review,* 21 April 1963, 27.

51. Martin Price, "New Books in Review," *Yale Review* 52 (June 1963), 602–4.

52. Harriet de Onís to William Koshland, 23 March 1966.

53. Alexander Coleman, "Thinking Beasts," *New York Times Book Review,* 17 April 1966, 5.

54. William Grossman, "A Mystic Light in the Backlands," *Saturday Review of Literature*, 16 April 1966, 44.

55. Vincent, *João Guimarães Rosa,* 71.

56. Harriet de Onís to Herbert Weinstock, 22 November 1967.

57. Harriet de Onís to Alfred Knopf, April 1966.

58. Barbara Shelby to Alfred Knopf, 16 December 1966.

59. Alexander Coleman, "Magnets Inside," *New York Times Book Review,* 29 September 1968, 4.

60. Barbara Shelby to Alfred Knopf, 16 February 1967.

61. Ibid., 28 June 1967.

62. Barbara Shelby, "Introduction," *The Third Bank of the River: Other Stories by J. G. Rosa* (New York: Alfred A. Knopf, 1968), v–x.

63. Alfred Knopf to Elinor Halle, 9 February 1970.

64. W. Trask, Editorial Report on *The Apple in the Dark*, 12 July 1963.

65. Alfred Knopf to Barbara Shelby, 29 March 1966.

66. Gregory Rabassa to Herbert Weinstock, 16 March 1965.

67. Ibid., 5 November 1965.

68. Gregory Rabassa, "Introduction," *The Apple in the Dark* by Clarice Lispector (New York: Alfred A. Knopf, 1967), xii.

69. Herbert Weinstock to Gregory Rabassa, 7 February 1966.

70. C. D. B. Bryan, "Afraid To Be Afraid," *New York Times Book Review,* 3 September 1967, 22.

71. Richard Frank Goldman, "Deeds in the Mind," *Saturday Review of Literature*, 19 August 1967, 48.

72. Franco, *Spanish American Literature*, 314.

73. Herbert Weinstock to J. B. Priestley, 7 December 1966.

74. William Styron to Herbert Weinstock, 26 July 1956.

75. Ralph Ellison to Herbert Weinstock, 21 June 1956.

76. Dorothy Van Ghent, "New Books in Review," *Yale Review* 46 (winter 1957), 275.

77. Selden Rodman, "Journey into the Night," *New York Times Book Review,* 14 October 1956, 5.

78. Herbert Weinstock, "Letters to the Editor," *New York Times Book Review,* 4 November 1956, 44; and Selden Rodman, "Letters to the Editor," 18 November 1956, 56.

79. Herbert Weinstock to Alejo Carpentier, 31 August 1956.

80. Ibid., 5 August 1957.

81. Phoebe Adams, "Alejo Carpentier's *The Kingdom of This World,*" *Atlantic Monthly,* August 1957, 84–85.

82. Angus Cameron, Letter of Recommendation for José Donoso's Guggenheim application, April 1967.

83. Alexander Coleman, "The Dictatorship of Senility," *New York Times Book Review,* 14 March 1965, 5.

84. Angus Cameron to Carl Brandt, 8 December 1966.

85. Ibid.

86. José Donoso to Angus Cameron, January 1967.

87. Ibid., 27 April 1967.

88. Ibid., 20 July 1967.

89. Ibid., 17 March 1967.

90. Ibid., 20 July 1967.

91. Kurt Vonnegut to Angus Cameron, 20 August 1967.

92. Alfred Knopf to Angus Cameron, 26 January 1967.

93. Robert Coover, "The Obscene Bird of Night," *New York Times Book Review,* 17 June 1973, 1–2.

94. Michael Wood, "Where the Wolf Howls," *New York Review of Books,* 13 December 1973, 19–22.

95. Alfred Knopf to Barbara Shelby, 25 January 1966.

96. Alfred Knopf to Jean Franco, 3 December 1969.

3

The Plumed Horn/ El Corno Emplumado: The Spell of Cuba in the 1960s

Waldo Frank and Blanche and Alfred Knopf wished to get a hearing for their Latin American authors from the New York literary establishment. However, with the proliferation of little magazines in the sixties, new alternatives for the diffusion of Latin American writing emerged. Little magazine editors were more adventurous than the former crusaders for Latin writing. They actively sought young, experimental writers and focused on poetry, a more difficult genre to market. Among the most prominent of the "littles" that turned to Latin America in the sixties was *The Plumed Horn/El Corno Emplumado.*

The bilingual magazine was edited in Mexico City by an inter-American couple—New York poet Margaret Randall and Mexican poet Sergio Mondragón. Together, as long as their marriage lasted, they struggled to create a link between the younger generation of poets and artists of the two Americas. Despite its limited circulation (an average of 3,000 copies), the quarterly succeeded in forging close ties with avant-garde groups and their publications throughout the hemisphere. The magazine established what Randall identified as the "common need to know what was happening to the North, what was happening to the South,"[1] in the area of poetry.

I

Randall's fascination with Latin America and Mondragón's attraction to the American avant-garde had their roots in the emergence of the Beat generation in the fifties. Like their predecessors in the twenties, a younger generation of American writers and artists undertook pilgrimages to Mexico in the late forties and fifties. Mexico provided an alternative to the values and mores of the American middle class they sought to escape. Its appeal rested in its suggestion of a new, unconventional way of life. As the writer LeRoi Jones put it: "We go to Mexico for a vacation. The place is a haven for bearded young men of my generation to go and make their 'scene.' "[2] The cast of regular visitors to Mexico included Allen Ginsberg and his fellow Beats, Jack Kerouac, William Burroughs, and Lawrence Ferlinghetti; San Franciscan poet Philip Lamantia; and Charles Olson, a Black Mountain poet and critic. In addition to discontented Americans, Mexico had lured avant-garde writers from Latin America, such as Nicaraguan Ernesto Cardenal and Peruvian Raquel Jodorowsky. It was to this mixed community that the young Margaret Randall came in 1961. Her motives for leaving New York fit neatly with the spirit of revolt that drew this group of artists together: "I left New York and arrived in Mexico City with my small son; with a still to some extent individualized anguish, a consequently off-center rage, and the determination that everything would be different. . . . My spiritual baggage: middle class and provincial America, an awakening in the Beat fifties. . . . Politics: progressive but unorganized; indignant but baffled."[3]

The meeting place for this bohemian inter-American community was Philip Lamantia's flat in downtown Mexico City. At the gatherings everybody would read his latest poem to the accompaniment of jazz. Looking back, Randall observed that the value of this coming together stemmed from the questions asked over and over: "What did we, from the North, know of Vallejo, of Neruda, much less the expression of our more contemporary Latin American brothers and sisters? What did these poets and writers, whose medium was Spanish, know of our Williams, Pound, Creeley, Blackburn?" [4]

The launching of *The Plumed Horn* in late 1961 was an attempt to answer those questions. Above all, Randall and Mondragón wanted to provide a forum for discussion and acquaintance among poets and little magazine devotees throughout the Americas. The very name of the quarterly attested to their staunch inter-American commitment. *The Plumed Horn/El Corno Emplumado* symbolized the jazz horn of the United States and the plumes of Quetzalcoatl, a tribute to both the contemporary and the pre-Columbian cultures of the Americas.

The magazine partook of the spirit of the sixties. It was anti-academic and fiercely devoted to helping new writers. Like its counterparts in the United States, the magazine demonstrated a remarkable ability for absorbing diverse political and social concerns. Randall and Mondragón operated *The Plumed Horn* as a clearinghouse for Orientalism, drugs, anti-war activism, and "hipness." Yet, if most editors prided themselves on having "a definite literary bone to pick," Randall and Mondragón did not.[5] They welcomed any writer provided his or her work exuded an anti-establishment flavor. As the editorial note of the first issue stated: "[This will be] a magazine of poetry, prose, letters, art from two hemispheres . . . whose pages conform to the word . . . now, when relations between the Americas have never been worse, we hope *El Corno Emplumado* will be a showcase (outside politics); for the fact that WE ARE ALL BROTHERS."[6]

The content of this issue faithfully reflected this lofty sentiment. It brought together Philip Lamantia's "Contra Satanus," Ernesto Cardenal's historical poem "El Estrecho Dudoso," and shorter poems by Raquel Jodorowsky, New Yorker Rochelle Owens, and the editors. It also carried an article by Mexican anthropologist Laurette Sejourne on the ruins of Monte Albán and original drawings by Elaine de Kooning and Milton Resnick. The editors' eclecticism discomfited some of their readers. This made it difficult to collect materials and to persuade contributors that the magazine was going to survive. Issue number two was definitely more focused on poetry in translation. Randall and Mondragón translated sections of Ginsberg's *Howl* (1956) and thus made the Beat poet available for the first time in Spanish. The editor's mother, Elinor Randall, translated Cesar Vallejo's "Retablo," which was, likewise, one of the earliest versions of the Peruvian's work to appear in English. Other contributors were the poets Robert Creeley, Paul Blackburn, Robert Kelly, and Mexican Rosario Castellanos.

Latin American readers greeted the magazine with great enthusiasm. It attracted writers from different camps who were exhilarated to be able to read their idols Ginsberg and Ferlinghetti in Spanish. As a reader remarked, the magazine's Beat proclivities agreed with the aesthetic concerns of a number of younger Latin American writers in the sixties: "Es la primera revista verdaderamente beatnik que se pone al alcance del lector hispanoamericano." [It is the first truly beatnik magazine to reach Latin American readers.][7]

In the United States the impact of the first issues was quite the opposite from which Randall hoped. Readers charged that the magazine was poorly produced or simply too lax in its standards. Some, like the poet and translator Clayton Eshelman, even argued that being far from New York or San Francisco, *The Plumed Horn* was vulnerable to poor treatment from American contributors. He claimed that she was getting second-rate material from a number of good American poets.[8]

Despite its sluggish beginnings, the arrival of *The Plumed Horn* in American culture was timely. With the decline of the cold war consensus and the rise of youthful political protest, interest in Latin America was starting to emerge. If in the forties this interest had been officially promoted, this time it was tied to anti-establishment feelings. Cuba's leader, Fidel Castro, proved himself capable of moving artists, intellectuals, and students to ecstatic identification with his goals. Critic Morris Dickstein wrote that Castro "in his pre-Leninist phase was another of our idols: the compleat [*sic*] hippie revolutionary."[9] The Cuban experiment represented a popular social cause, a new society open to thought and creativity.

Among leftists and the artistic avant-garde support for Castro was strong. The Fair Play for Cuba Committee was founded in the spring of 1960. It opened chapters on many campuses and sponsored trips to Cuba to allow a firsthand view of the revolutionary regime. Many of those who traveled to Havana hardly spoke Spanish and knew little about Latin America. Cuban novelist Guillermo Cabrera Infante, now exiled in London, drew a colorful picture of this brand of tourism. Recalling the celebration of July 26 in the Sierra Maestra mountains in 1960, he wrote: "[Susan Sontag] was in Cuba in 1960. . . . Among many others present at this fiesta were LeRoi Jones and Francoise Sagan. . . . LeRoi Jones was wearing very different clothes from his present . . . uniform—a suit of raw silk, cut in the English style, and Italian shoes, and he smoked Gauloises all the time. . . . His gestures, like his clothes, suggested dandyism rather than revolution, and were, of course, decidedly European."[10]

By mid-1960 the first interpretations of the revolution by these visitors began to appear. Jones, for example, lavishly described his pilgrimage to the Sierra Maestra in *The Evergreen Review*. His equation of Fidel's eloquence to that of an ancient bard showed his entrancement. A year later Norman Mailer wrote in *The Village Voice* an open letter to the Cuban leader and thanked him for helping create "a new and better mood which has been coming to America."[11] From traditional leftist quarters and academia came Leo Huberman and Paul Sweezy's *Cuba, Anatomy of a Revolution* (1961), C. Wright Mill's *Listen, Yankee* (1960), and dozens of laudatory articles in journals like *Studies on the Left* and *Dissent*. The Cuban euphoria spilled over to literary publications as well. LeRoi Jones's *Yugen* and *The Northwest Review* ran long interviews with Castro in 1961 and the fall of 1963, respectively. Most accounts failed utterly to discern the totalitarian proclivities of their hero. As critic Dennis Wrong pointed out: "Some of Castro's New Left supporters in the United States seem in an equally short time to have traveled from a fresh rebellious idealism . . . to a fascination with populist totalitarianism that is scarcely distinguishable from that of the latter-day Communist apologists of the late 30's and early 40's."[12]

Thanks to Cuba, Latin American culture enjoyed a vogue of popularity in the early sixties. In the area of literature the "littles" led the way. *The Evergreen Review* devoted its 1959 winter issue to Mexican writers. Edited by critic Donald Allen and with translations by the poet Lysander Kemp, the number included, among many pieces, an excerpt from Octavio Paz's *The Labyrinth of Solitude* (1950), chapters of Juan Rulfo's *Pedro Páramo* (1955), and Carlos Fuentes's "The Life Line." There were also special Latin American issues of *Texas Quarterly*, *New World Writing*, and the Manhattan based newspaper *P'Alante*. Foremost among those who turned south was poet Robert Bly, editor of *The Sixties* and founder of The Sixties Press. Bly had come across the work of Neruda and Vallejo while living in Norway in the late fifties. He was immediately won over and went so far as to declare that the greatest poetry in this century had been written in Spanish. This statement, of course, has to be read in the context of the revolt against the New Criticism that was coming to full strength in the early sixties. From San Francisco to North Carolina, where Olson led the Black Mountain movement, younger poets rejected the New Critics' emphasis on irony, ambiguity, and impersonality. They abandoned what they deemed to be an excessive concern with form and brought the self back to the center of their work. Bly's fascination with the inner workings of his psyche attuned him to the sensibility of Spanish and Latin American surrealism. He admired Neruda, Vallejo, and Federico García Lorca's "marvelous intensity" and capacity to probe deep into the unconscious.[13] Furthermore, the Latin Americans' concern with creating politically engaged work that sprang from inner sources appeared to him to be an effective antidote to the New Critics' disdain for ideology: "Once a poet takes a political stand, the wise also assure us that he will cease writing good poetry. During the Spanish Civil War, Neruda became a Communist, and has remained one; most of his great books, one must admit, date after that time."[14]

Bly periodically published translations of works by Vallejo and Neruda in his magazine. He also edited an anthology containing the best

work of the two poets. In an essay written for that volume he urged fellow poets to inject their verse with Latin vitality: "Many poets we all
know are able to associate with considerable speed when there are not
many mammal emotions—Wallace Stevens, for example, creates a
philosophical calm in his poetry, inside of which he associates quite
rapidly—but when anger or anguish enter the poem they become tongue
tied, or lapse into clichés. Vallejo does just the opposite. Under the
pressure of powerful human feeling . . . he leaps about wildly, each
leap throwing him farther out into the edges of consciousness."[15]

Bly's efforts to make North Americans aware of Latin poetry, though
commendable, were limited in scope, for he only crusaded for established writers. *The Plumed Horn*, on the other hand, paid equal attention
to both established and newer writers. In addition, the magazine's close
ties with Latin American artists provided readers in the United States
with a richer picture of what was happening to the south than Bly's did.
Poet Kirby Congdon observed that Bly was on the inside looking out.
He wondered how he could really be in touch with Latin America when
he operated in Minnesota. He claimed that it had the ring of being chic
rather than involved.[16]

When it came to Cuba, *The Plumed Horn* offered the best coverage of
that country's cultural and political scene. In 1962, when President
Kennedy imposed a blockade against Cuba, most contacts with the island ended. Because Mexico maintained diplomatic ties with Havana,
Randall and Mondragón could easily communicate with Cuban intellectuals. They exchanged publications with the Cuban cultural institution
and publishing house Casa de las Américas and befriended Cuban cultural officials. Thus, their magazine became an invaluable source for
those Americans interested in keeping up with the revolutionary
regime.

Another feature that made the magazine stand out among those printing Latin American literature was Randall's determination to establish
an inter-American community of poets, a network that allowed exchanges ranging from homes to poetic theories. In 1964 Randall and
Mondragón organized the "First Encounter of American Poets" in Mexico City. Among those who participated or sent messages of support
were Thomas Merton, Lawrence Ferlinghetti, and Mexican poet Marco
Antonio Montes de Oca. To buttress this sense of poetic solidarity the
editors helped with plans for the construction of "La Casa del Hombre."
In tune with the longing for community so prevalent in the sixties, the
project entailed the building of a center where artists would live, work,

and be close to nature. The house would be located on the outskirts of Mexico City and be permanently open to artists of the two Americas. Though the plans fell through, Randall and Mondragón kept the idea alive. Indeed, their house became a rough approximation of the dream community. For Latin and American avant-garde poets and artists who went through Mexico City, their roomy home provided the obvious place to stay.

II

During the first years, the English and Spanish sections of the magazine shared identical editorial goals and philosophy. Nonetheless, each bore the mark of its editor. Margaret Randall was of course in charge of the North American part. Having come from New York and been a regular of the Cedar Bar in the East Village, she was imbued with the Beat and Black Mountain spirit. Like many of her generation, she worshipped a set of poets that included Pound, Williams, Ginsberg, and Robert Creeley. Randall's editorship displayed as well a taste for abstract expressionism, a style she had come to love after working in painter Red Grooms's studio in the late fifties. Thus, it was only natural that she would continue the eclecticism that had marked her own formation and allow, as Clayton Eshelman noted, "Catholic priests to commingle with Communist guerrillas" without thinking much of it.[17]

In a rambling declaration of poetic principles written for *Kulchur* in 1965, she expressed contempt for "poetic diction" and her devotion to an aesthetic that fused Ginsberg's wild imagery and confessional mode with Charles Olson's obsession with the "breath," poetry based on breathing and our natural rhythms: "So where is the line? where do we stand? what pattern, if any, can be made of the bits and pieces reeling across our present horizon? . . . We must begin with an honest eye/ear to the evidence before us. The beat rampage means nothing (except societally) but ginsberg's wild breath line, corso's modern imagery, lamantia's visionary religiosity and kerouac's new prosody do mean something—to anyone willing to read, listen, taking the trouble to wake his senses and learn."[18]

She was also interested in translation. Elsewhere in the *Kulchur* piece she acknowledged the impact of Neruda and Vallejo on North American poets: "'deep image' has shown a new link of form and content in a meaningful opening in, the depths of which I suspect have only begun to be tapped. The american poet has only to look beyond his national boundaries (there are other poets in the world, you know)."[19]

Though *The Plumed Horn* never had a paid staff, Randall managed to keep in touch with hundreds of poets and editors back home. She became the Latin American correspondent for the network of "littles." Often she would review Latin American poetry in translation for magazines like *Trace, Kulchur,* and poet Robert Kelly's *Trobar.* In 1963 she reviewed Muriel Ruykeyser's translation of *Sunstone* by Octavio Paz. The article, published in *Trace,* urged Americans to read Paz's "clear and moving epic."[20] She also served as literary agent for Latin American poets and persuaded North American editors to make room for their work. It was owing to her advocacy and pressure that Eshelman agreed to review Raquel Jodorowsky's *AJY TOJEN* for the fall 1965 issue of *Kulchur.* The long poem had appeared in *The Plumed Horn* that same year. Eshelman dismissed Randall's translation as "raw and straight" and "not exciting." Yet she was not discouraged. She even tried to interest the influential avant-garde editor Cid Corman in her Latin friends. As editor of *Origin,* Corman was disheartened by the quality of what was being printed in most "littles." When it came to modern Latin American writing he was outright negative. In 1966 he wrote: "For several years now I've been inundated with all kinds of hopeless publications and unofficial sources in Central and South America. . . . Would you kindly inform those people . . . that I cannot read Spanish without great labor and unless the literature is on the level of Vallejo and Lorca not to bother."[21]

Corman's coolness did not dampen her zeal. She strongly objected to any "misreading" of Latin American avant-garde work. When a critic chose to overlook a group of younger Colombian poets in an article published in *Trace,* Randall leaped to their defense: "When [he] gets to Colombia, he forgets the Nadaistas, that wild and woolly group responsible for much of what's alive artistically in that country. . . . Latin America is exploding in the arts, as in other ways, and I hate to see it superficially or badly interpreted."[22]

To the disaffected readers and editors of "littles" in the United States, Randall's messages from the south must have felt like a breath of fresh air. She reported that Latin America was bursting with art, experimentation, and rebellion. Her descriptions of life in Mexico City took on mystical overtones: "Mexico City . . . what can I say? It is a city of mystery and solitude and hundreds of underlying currents stemming from a mixture of cultures which at times seem to bridge East and

West. Coming from the last three years in New York—the intensity, action, that particular density which only New York has—I find it remote at times, strange, very beautiful, not terribly conducive to work (in the New York sense)."[23]

Randall managed to stir up interest in Latin American avant-garde literature among fellow U.S. poets at the same time that she encouraged their romantic visions of Hispanic culture. While Bly relied on South American voices to bring politics back into poetry, she espoused the idea that the American poetic tradition could be enlarged by looking beyond Neruda and Vallejo.

Randall also used the "littles" to find American poets who would appeal to her Latin audience. The poet Thomas Merton was one of her "finds" who developed quite a following in Latin America. The work of this Catholic monk and poet was well known in the United States when Randall published three of his poems in the spring 1963 issue of *The Plumed Horn*. Randall's selection included "A Picture of Lee Ying" and "Glose in the Sin of Ixion." These poems reflected Merton's increasing attraction to Zen and other Eastern religions. They were translated by Cuban poet Cintio Vitier. Later, in 1968, the magazine published Merton's "Studies of Man's Friendly Competitor The Rat Have Shown."

In the United States the Beat poets were fond of Merton's mysticism, his interest in Eastern religions, and his staunch commitment to peace. Latin Americans, on the other hand, respected his belief that a monk should understand the problems of the secular world. Merton's ideas were spelled out in the letters he wrote, from the Trappist monastery in Gethsemani, Kentucky, to the editors of *The Plumed Horn*. Often he commented on Latin American politics and the situation of Cuba in the late sixties: "I love Cuba, Cuban people. Not permitted in this country even to think of Cuba, still less of going to Cuba. Of course the thing is that when people are able to do something about deciding their own destiny they are relatively happy because they begin to become themselves. But also when a big fat people starts deciding everybody else's destiny then it becomes alienated by its own abuse of power, ceases to be anything but its own image of itself."[24]

His attack on American policy, however, was more a cry of moral outrage than outright support of Castro. Merton often disapproved of the overt politicizing so prevalent among Latin American writers. In a message to the readers of *The Plumed Horn*, he warned against the dangers of mixing art with politics: "When a Marxist poet writes only as a Marxist he ceases to write as a poet; and the result is so obvious it is laughable. . . . When will people discover that artistic truth and any other truth is never manufactured in the offices of bureaucrats or thought police?"[25]

Merton had been ahead of his time in reading Latin American literature. Through his friendship with Ernesto Cardenal, who had studied in Merton's monastery, he discovered Paz, Vallejo, and many other poets long before they were available in English. Like Bly, he believed North American poetry had lost its inventive force. The technological atmosphere surrounding the artist in the United States, he thought, had induced a "state of spiritual stupor" and left him unable to "really say anything."[26] He deemed it imperative to look to South America for inspiration. Merton was personally convinced that the best American poetry was written in Latin America. He thought that, besides Octavio Paz and a host of other Mexican and Central American poets, there were the great ones of a generation past, like Cesar Vallejo, who, in his opinion, was the poet of the century because he had the most to say. He felt that in Latin America the voice of the poet had significance because it had something to do with life.[27]

Aware that publishing the Beats strengthened the appeal of the magazine, Randall developed a solid bond with Ginsberg and with Ferlinghetti and his City Lights Press and Bookstore. The business end of the relationship left a lot to be desired. Often Ferlinghetti complained that the magazine did not sell well in San Francisco. Yet, for all his misgivings, he enjoyed the quarterly's fresh news from Latin America: "No. 10 is great . . . especially the drawings by Topor, the Indian primitive poetry and the Brazilian concretions."[28] Getting poetry from the Beats, however, was easier than having them promote the magazine. Ginsberg and Ferlinghetti traveled in South America. In 1962 they attended a writers' congress in Concepción, Chile and met Chilean poet Nicanor Parra, whose *Anti-Poems* (1960) were published by City Lights. Consequently, they supported the magazine's inter-American outlook and willingly allowed Randall to translate their work. In addition to *Howl*, *The Plumed Horn* published Ginsberg's *Kaddish* (1961) in a translation by Mexican poet Ernesto de la Peña in 1966.

Though Ginsberg never contributed original work to the magazine, he was friendly and helpful to it and to Randall, as reporter Jane Kramer found him to be toward everyone in his life.[29] He was the "avuncular" master who dazzled readers of *The Plumed Horn* with the letters sent from the Orient: "I got to India and am in the Himalayas talking to naked Saddhiis and Tibetan Lamas with Gary Snyder and Peter Orlovsky and we don't have dysentery and India is the most—a super Mexico."[30]

Ferlinghetti was more generous with his poetry. For the January 1963 issue he sent his "Tirade for C. W. Mills," a tribute to the leftist sociologist and supporter of Castro. Alluding to the failed Bay of Pigs invasion of Cuba in 1961, Ferlinghetti wrote: "Good night sweet prince Kennedy . . . and good day Ginsberg and good day Fidel. He doesn't want to marry your sister. He just wants to socialize."[31] In 1964 Randall ran his "The Great Chinese Dragon" in a translation by Chilean critic and writer Fernando Alegría and, in number 29, "The Third World," as a posthumous homage to Che Guevara.

From 1962 through 1966, the last issue of each year was devoted to the work of a single poet. In October 1963, it focused on Robert Kelly's *Her Body Against Time*, printed in English and Spanish. Kelly's "deep imagism," like Randall's, was rooted in the teachings of Olson and in Spanish and Latin American surrealism. Kelly's intricate poetry was translated by Randall and Mondragón. Their work was that rarity among translations—a pleasure to the original author. Kelly wrote: "Please, please be at ease about the translations: what you've done already, what I've seen, is so right you have no grounds to worry."[32]

In addition to *Her Body Against Time*, Randall and Mondragón published a long list of Kelly's poems. Among the best were "Poem for February" and "The Mayan Poem," which captured Kelly's fascination with pre-Columbian cultures.

As editor of *Trobar*, Kelly was sympathetic to the economic woes affecting *The Plumed Horn*. After hearing that in 1964 Randall and Mondragón had sold the furniture from their apartment to pay for an issue, he sent his condolences and encouragement: "You must know from some itinerant astrologer or other that you have Neptune and Moon conjunction at midheaven, which would be one poor, old tired system's way of predicting your power of vitality, life magically summoning life into things, the way a Navajo in his ceremonies will summon a god into the rock or into that tree."[33]

Other Black Mountain writers published in *The Plumed Horn* included Robert Creeley, Paul Blackburn, and Ed Dorn. Of the three, Creeley's work was the hardest to obtain. He maintained that he had no time to write something original for the magazine and little unpublished work available. Over a seven-year span, Randall won from him the right to publish only three of his minimalist poems.

Paul Blackburn, on the other hand, developed a close relationship with the magazine. His experience in France as a Fulbright lecturer and two years in Spain had made him aware of the importance of translation. As poetry editor for the *Nation* (1961–1966) and a translator himself, he welcomed the influx of poetry coming from South America. Though he considered the quality of Randall and Mondragón's translations to be "uneven," he quickly warmed up to the journal.[34] He told Randall that the second issue (April 1962) had given him great heart for the project and that it seemed they were truly getting down to business.[35] As evidence of his faith he submitted "The Limitation" for the third issue, and two other poems for number six. Later in 1966, the magazine printed a large selection of his work in bilingual form. Blackburn's most valuable contribution to the magazine, however, was his solicitous attitude and his legwork in Greenwich Village rounding up an audience for the benefit readings to keep the publication alive.

Ed Dorn was even closer to the magazine. He shared both Randall's increasingly leftist leanings and Mondragón's penchant for psychedelic drugs. In 1966 he wrote from Lebanon: "Anyway I'm sending you some poems which are a kind of journal of things running through the time. I wouldn't know how to pin them down. . . . Admittedly I'm uneasy about the verbal exoticism of hashish which is behind all this."[36]

Dorn's political leanings showed themselves in poems like "Sportscasts Colonialism," which Randall and Mondragón translated into Spanish. Appropriately, the poem appeared in number 26 of the magazine, which had a Cuban poster on the cover.

Dorn used the magazine as a bridge to Latin America. Through Randall, he became acquainted with the work of Mexican poet José Emilio Pacheco and revolutionary poets from Peru and Central America and managed, as he put it, to move beyond "the obvious people, Neruda, Vallejo, etc."[37] He also shared the editor's excitement over Cuba. As late as 1967, he was still clinging to the vision of Cuba as the last Edenic outpost: "Again one does get the feeling of great vitality and freedom. . . . What better refutation of all the U.S. propaganda against 'socialist totalitarianism.'"[38]

Diane Wakoski had a good deal in common with the three Black Mountain poets. Like them, she revered Williams's and Olson's call for poetry to cast aside traditional culture and syntax and find in the "unmediated self" the principle of form.[39] Of all the American poets Randall lured to *The Plumed Horn*, she was perhaps the one who contributed the best work. In 1963 her "But the map was everything" appeared; a bilingual version of "Sun"—translated by the editors—followed in 1964; and in 1966 came her now well-known long poem, "George Washington: The Father of My Country." By 1967 Randall had exposed readers to a broad spectrum of younger American poets. From New York to San Francisco and from Ginsberg to Jerome Rothenberg and LeRoi Jones, she had included most of the figures Donald M. Allen brought together in his seminal *The New American Poetry: 1945–1960* (1960).

The large group of poets who contributed to *The Plumed Horn* appreciated the opportunity of being translated into Spanish and learning about Latin American literature. This service, however, was not always met without criticism. Denise Levertov and Robert Bly, for example, distrusted the magazine's catholic tastes and avoided collaborating with it. Levertov's main quibble was the editors' tendency to print a great number of letters praising their efforts: "I have sometimes been irritated by a certain pervasive tone that seems to me somewhat hysterical, and by the self-congratulatory and mutual back-slapping that goes on in the letter section. . . . What I call hysteria is an attitude of fervent poetic brotherhood which, while I am in sympathy with the desires that give rise to it, seems to be more than a little inflated."[40]

But Levertov did more than lament Randall's editorship. She used the magazine's letter section to condemn fellow artists who did not share her anti-war sentiments. In 1966 she launched an attack against poet Ted Enslin. In contrast to most sixties artists, Enslin believed that a poet had "better things to do than to try to repair the so-called 'big' concerns of the world," which he deemed "at best pretty hollow."[41] In a letter to Randall, printed in 1965 without his permission, he lapsed deeper into the subject of non-involvement and complained about the magazine's "tinge of pink." These remarks sparked Levertov's anger, which she vented in a letter made public in number 19: "To sneer at 'political awareness' is so silly it defies comment, except to say that if only more people were politically aware we would not now be in the midst of this hellish mess."[42] Being herself an activist, she defended politically engaged writing: "[It is] the work of writers intelligent and whole enough to understand that the poet has no exclusive area of concern. . . . There is no danger, no shame, and no hope, in which we are not all involved."[43]

As for Robert Bly's misgivings, they focused on the Beat emphasis, which had been so heavy in the early issues. He cautioned Randall against serving worn-out leftovers. He said that the poetry of people like Lamantia was almost too bad to be believed.[44]

Clayton Eshelman often disapproved of Randall's excessive tolerance. Despite the fact that he regularly sent both his poems and his translations of Vallejo and Neruda, he hoped the editors would feature more Robert Duncan or Louis Zukofsky, whom he considered to be the best voices of the avant-garde. He said he did not understand why Randall would break her back to print some of the authors she did.[45]

Randall's editorship was a constant struggle to bridge the gap between poetry and the streets. Often this resulted in a mixed array of materials ranging from *Kaddish* to astrology and urban uprisings. This approach gave readers in both Americas a sense of the changes these cultures were undergoing. Like many others of the time, Randall perceived the decade as a time to cast off old values in politics, art, and sexuality. She contended that the sixties were a time of mad explosion, as she described the era in the editorial note of the third issue: "Our age—Cuba, Africa, Chessman [Caryl Chessman, the California death row inmate who became a culture hero of the Left], A–Bombs, civil disobedience, abstract expressionism, electronic music, a million babies born every day—compresses the history we wake to a madness which has fractured the light in which we move."[46]

Ultimately, what characterized the first four years of the magazine was a loosely defined humanism. *The Plumed Horn*'s editorials, though suffused with political overtones, remind one more of a mild anarchism than of doctrinaire socialism. Pleas for the "agrarian reform of the soul" and salutes to the "new man" and the age of Aquarius took precedence over political advice. When during this issue the magazine embraced a political cause, it was to protest censorship or the arrests of fellow editors charged with obscenity. In 1964 the editors supported those who marched through Greenwich Village to protest the "harassment of the arts" following the arrest of Ed Sanders, editor of the underground porno-art journal *Fuck You.*[47] Typical of the non-poetic sections of the magazine during this period were reports of life in New York City by poet Carol Berge. A sense of what Morris Dickstein later called the "romantic excess"[48] of the era permeates her prose: "Plenty of all kinds of action, any kind you want here: art, drugs, theatre, fuzz, Ukrainians next to hippies, egg cream and Ratners's and Khadeja's African fabric boutique, a barber shop with a stripy pole and a new magic parlor near it where you spend double and come out four—times more than—Carnaby."[49]

Other letters Randall published reveal that the decade's obsession with self-liberation and "heightened awareness" was not confined to the cities. Though many artists proclaimed their disenchantment with the Vietnam War by staging marches and sit-ins, an important group boycotted the establishment through utter withdrawal. This pastoral impulse—which may have seemed puzzling to Latin Americans used to thinking of U.S. culture in urban terms—was best displayed in Enslin's letters. From his retreat in Maine he would write: "And this morning I shot a porcupine in the cellar. No middle men! And that is how I like to live, cutting my own fuel, making clothes."[50]

The Plumed Horn was eclectic also in its coverage of the visual arts scene. While Mondragón attracted the collaboration of Mexican painters like José Luis Cuevas and Carlos Topor, Randall obtained that of Elaine de Kooning, Marc di Suvero, and other figures identified with the second generation of abstract expressionism and with pop art. The editors would print reviews—often eyewitness accounts of the latest art events in New York. In 1966 the artist Eleanor Antin described a "happening" Allen Kaprow staged for his friends in Long Island: "It was like Moses leading the people . . . or some other such grand event. I like to think of Allen Kaprow as our Cecil B. de Mille [*sic*] creating spectaculars just for us and besides he looks like Jesus."[51]

While pieces like this provided the reader with a glimpse of the experimentalism shaking the art scene, there was no editorial guidance as to how to interpret these "happenings." But a more analytical approach went against the grain of the magazine, which, like most of the "littles" of the sixties, prided itself on valuing self-expression and spontaneity over intellectualism and thought-out criticism.

III

While Randall's editorial choices seldom ventured beyond Beat and Black Mountain poets, Mondragón's were more varied. Under his editorship, the Spanish section encompassed poets as different in attitude and craft as Paz, Ernesto Cardenal, and the belated Colombian Dadaist Gonzalo Arango. Aware of the poor publishing and distribution conditions in Latin America—most writers did not know what was happening in the neighboring countries—he attempted to make *The Plumed Horn* a point where the different currents of poetry flourishing in the hemisphere would converge.

When the magazine appeared in 1962, most of the "classic" figures of Spanish American poetry had already begun to find their way into English. Undoubtedly, Mondragón had no qualms about featuring their work, but his efforts were mainly directed at giving an outlet to young avant-garde poets who had seldom been published.

The Plumed Horn's access to the United States gave it a privileged position in the circuit of Latin American "littles," which extended from Mexico City to Buenos Aires and included such publications as the Argentine *Eco Contemporáneo* and *Airón*, the Venezuelan *El Techo de la Ballena*, the Chilean *Orfeo*, and the Mexican *Pájaro Cascabel*.

Mondragón's section received many contributions. A significant portion came from poets who late in the seventies were widely recognized and translated. A case in point is that of Ernesto Cardenal, who in the early sixties was scarcely known outside of Nicaragua. Cardenal sympathized with the magazine's ignoring of writers' cliques and applauded their penchant for experimentation. In its early years he envisioned the magazine as an outlet for those poets who wanted to cast off the spell of Neruda and high-flown rhetoric. Poets like Nicanor Parra and his fellow Chilean Enrique Lihn, for instance, sought new forms of expression through the use of colloquial language and parody of tradition. In this context Cardenal encouraged the editors to support younger poets:

Supongo que seguirán ustedes agitando México. Agitarán también toda América Latina si continúan el trabajo, es necesario crear un movimiento renovador, acabar con la complacencia, la literatura consagrada, la retórica que se ha impuesto, las consignas, las conspiraciones del silencio.

[I guess you will continue to stir up Mexico. If you continue with your work, you will stir up all Latin America. It is necessary to create a fresh movement, to end complacency, established literature, rhetoric, passwords, and the conspiracies of silence.][52]

The humanist rhetoric also appealed to Cardenal, a would-be monk. In a rapture of romanticism, he backed "La Casa de Hombre" project and promoted the creation of a Pan-American union of poets. He asserted that the failure of the Organization of American States (OAS) had inspired poets to come up with their own version of inter-Americanism based on art rather than politics.

Cardenal's contributions to *The Plumed Horn* were multiple. He submitted poetry, translated from the English, and served as a link to other poets and publications. In addition to short poems, he sent longer poems, like "La Noche" and "Apocalipsis," which were written in the vein of Ezra Pound's *Cantos*. In 1966 the magazine published "Hora Cero," one of his most famous poems. Translated by British poet Donald Gardner, the poem appeared in bilingual form for the first time in the magazine.

Cardenal was well acquainted with modern American poetry. He believed that reading Williams and Ginsberg would have a liberating effect on the language of the younger generation of Latin American writers. *The Plumed Horn* was, he thought, the best vehicle to disseminate American poetry in Spanish America. With his friend, Nicaraguan José Coronel Urtecho, he translated some of Pound's *Cantos* and his haiku "In a Station of the Metro," which Mondragón ran in issue number 24. The following issue brought out his versions of Williams's "The Red Wheelbarrow" and "The Dance."

Cardenal was also instrumental in originating new projects for the magazine. In addition to participating in benefit readings, he was largely responsible for the selection of established and young Nicaraguan poets that appeared in 1963. In the spring 1964 issue, he guest edited a "small anthology" that introduced works of Eskimo, Iroquois, and Quechua poets. By late 1965, however, he had lost his initial enthusiasm. Mondragón's increasing attraction to the modish poetry of Colombian and Venezuelan avant-gardists did not suit Cardenal's ideas of genuine linguistic renovation. Infuriated by one of the editor's own surreal poems, he disparaged the magazine's fascination with obscurity:

Ya otra vez el año pasado te había dicho que creía que la poesía debía ser entendida por el pueblo, y que no se iba a ninguna parte con esa poesía de puro disparate, hermetismo y surrealismo transnochado. Me contestaste diciéndome que la poesía del *Corno* si el pueblo no la entendía ahora ya la entendería alguna vez. Bueno, pues yo no lo creo. . . . La poesía que no comunica no es nada.

[Once again last year I told you that I believed poetry must be understood by the people. Gibberish, hermetism, and worn-out surrealism does not lead anywhere. You replied that, if the people did not understand *El Corno* poetry now, they would later. . . . Well, I do not believe you. . . . Poetry that cannot communicate is nothing.][53]

In hindsight, it seems ironic that Cardenal, who later became the minister of culture in revolutionary Nicaragua, also disapproved of the blatantly political poetry that appeared in the magazine. He admonished the editors to steer away from radicalism of any sort. Before he became interested in liberation theology, Cardenal held a surprisingly critical view of Marxist regimes—in particular of Castro's bias against the arts:

No somos como los marxistas en todas partes, intransigentes, deshonestos, inmorales, silenciadores de todo lo que no es de la ideología de ellos (con la ideología de ellos todo, contra la ideología de ellos Nada). Yo los conozco muy bien (he tenido amistad con ellos en América durante 20 años y son— con algunas excepciones inmorales).

[We are not like the Marxists everywhere: intolerant, dishonest, immoral, and trying to silence anything that does not agree with their ideology (with their ideology everything, but against it Nothing). I know them well (I have had Marxist friends for 20 years and, with a few exceptions, they are immoral).][54]

Cardenal's warnings suggest the extent to which the editors were prone to be seduced by the trappings of the counterculture and the New Left. As the decade progressed, Randall became increasingly involved with the Cuban regime, and Mondragón started plunging deeper into Oriental mysticism, the occult, and assorted hallucinatory drugs. Cardenal feared that Mondragón's "spiritualist" tendency would wind up destroying both the credibility of the magazine and his brain: "Te doy este consejo serio: abandona pronto todo Esoterismo, Teosofía y Ocultismo. Estas tres cosas son sumamente perniciosas. Entontecen. Ya no podrás pensar. Tu mente sera un caos, te perderás como poeta, escritor y todo." [I am giving you this serious bit of advice: Forget esoterism, theosophy, and occultism. These three things are extremely harmful. You won't be able to think. Your mind will turn chaotic. You will be lost as a poet, a writer, and everything else.][55]

While the Nicaraguan distrusted Mondragón's inclinations, a group of younger Argentine poets led by Miguel Grinberg heartily cheered him on. Known as the "generación mufada" [the bad-tempered generation], these poets were swayed in the inter-American spirit fostered by the magazine. In support of Mondragón's "New Man" rhetoric and advocacy of fraternity among poets, they founded the movement "Nueva Solidaridad" and the little journal *Eco Contemporáneo*. The magazine's editorials evoked Mondragón's infatuation with "la revolución espiritual de la conciencia contemporánea" [the spiritual revolution of contemporary consciousness].[56]

Grinberg brought *The Plumed Horn* into contact with a number of Argentine writers, among them Julio Cortázar and younger poets. In 1963 Mondragón published a selection of new Argentine poetry. This sampling, which included forty-seven poets, was among the most successful of the anthologies devoted to a single country that the magazine published. It smoothly accommodated modern established figures like Alberto Girri with such lesser known poets as Alejandra Pizarnik. Her work appealed to American readers, who found echoes of Emily Dickinson in her "Revelaciones" and "Amantes." Soon after her poems appeared in the journal she became Mondragón's good friend. Unlike the older poet Eduardo Garavaglia, who lamented the exclusion of Oliverio Girondo and other twenties vanguardists,[57] Pizarnik commended Mondragón's balanced choice: "Estuve pensando que es una gran cosa que usted esté fuera de la Argentina, pues eso le ha permitido acercar poetas muy dispares." [I was think it's good that you are outside of Argentina. It has allowed you to bring together different poets.][58]

Unfortunately, the relationship the magazine established with avantgarde groups in Venezuela and Colombia was far more constricting. Mondragón's connection to the poets associated with *El Techo de la Ballena* prevented *The Plumed Horn* from gaining access to the more moderate writers grouped around the magazines *Zona Franca* and *Sardio.* Furthermore, the work of those linked to *El Techo*—Ludovico Silva, Edmundo Aray—was propagandistic and of little artistic value.

In Colombia, Mondragón befriended the "nadaista" poets. The movement had been started by Gonzalo Arango in the early sixties. Arango and his strident followers wanted to revive the iconoclastic stance of European Dadaism. Like the Dadaists, they assaulted established notions of art: "En vista de que nadie hace nada ... en vista de que estamos hartos de hacer literatura ... Los Nadaistas resolvemos decir ¡Basta! a estas sublimes porquerías." [Since nobody does anything ... since we're fed up with literature ... the Nadaistas have resolved to say "Enough!" of sublime rubbish.][59] The group also organized events that recalled raucous Dada demonstrations. The "Segundo Festival de Vanguardia" Arango set up in Cali in 1963 is a good example: "Espectáculos—desafíos a montón. La burgesía echando chispas una vez más, excomulgándonos. Entre lo mejor, conferencias de todos contra todos. 'Filosofía y Pollo Asado' por el Monje Loco." [Performances and all sorts of assaults. The establishment once again fuming and excommunicating us. Among the best lectures by everybody against everybody. "Philosophy and Fried Chicken" by the Mad Monk.][60]

The Nadaistas added little to *The Plumed Horn.* Their work was derivative and, as many readers argued, even lacking in shock value. In allotting too much space to their manifestos, Mondragón failed to give Colombian writing fair coverage.

When the magazine focused on Peru, its approach was sounder. Above all, Mondragón wanted to make American readers aware of Cesar Vallejo. Like Bly, he saw the Peruvian's work as the source of new Latin American writing, the creator of a genuinely South American language. He willingly collaborated with Clayton Eshelman on his translation of *Poemas humanos* (1938). Eshelman's translations appeared for the first time in *The Plumed Horn.* Later, in 1966, they were published by New Directions.

Vallejo's disjointed syntax and disconcerting imagery aroused Mondragón to a point that he had difficulty appreciating Peruvian poets who consciously removed themselves from the master. Undoubtedly what attracted him to the work of Raquel Jodorowsky was the hint of Vallejo in her style. The issue of October 1964 was solely devoted to her *AJY TOJEN*, which the editors translated into English. Her experimental verse and her delving into Andean myths excited readers throughout the hemisphere. Artists as different as Bly, Eshelman, and Cuevas applauded Mondragón's discovery. Walter Loewenfels, a poet of the old guard, wrote from New Jersey: "[She is] a self I have not heard since Vallejo died in 1938, [Paul] Eluard in 1956."[61]

In 1966 the magazine ran a small anthology of younger Peruvian poets. Critic Julio Ortega and Clayton Eshelman, then living in Lima, made the selections. Despite the fact that Eshelman deplored Ortega's omission of Blanca Varela, he persuaded Mondragón to go along with the critic's choices. He thought that it looked pretty good and that it might be one of their best for it was done within the country by a young interested poet who was in contact with many people.[62] Indeed, Ortega included some of the best new figures, like Manuel Scorza and Antonio Cisneros, who were brought to American attention for the first time in *The Plumed Horn.*

In his dealing with Chilean poetry, Mondragón was equally eclectic. He regularly made available, both in English and Spanish, the work of Neruda. He also came up with engaging assortments for the small anthology section of number 21 and featured Parra, Lihn, and Oscar Hahn. As with the young Peruvians, these last two poets were first introduced to American readers by the magazine.

By 1966 the small anthology section focusing on a single country was an institution. Whereas most of these samplings had been partially bilingual, the Mexican selection was fully translated into English. The magazine had its widest readership in Mexico and had been generously supported by grants from the Mexican government.

In Mexico City, Randall and Mondragón were identified with that clique of poets who worshipped the Beats and the American counterculture. When working on the Mexican anthology, however, they shunned these allegiances. As a result they produced a selection that encompassed the best of Mexican poetry since "Los Contemporáneos" in the late twenties. The editors hoped to stir up interest in Mexican poetry among American readers. They asked poets Jerome Rothenberg and Stephen Schwarz to translate the complex work of Isabel Fraire and Monte de Oca. Those who like Pacheco and Rosario Castellanos used a more traditional language were translated by Randall and her mother.

While younger poets saw their appearance in *The Plumed Horn* as a way to reach U.S. publishers, some established writers—notably Octavio Paz—were reluctant to be published in the magazine. Irked by the journal's reputation for uneven translations, Paz submitted four poems, but made their publication conditional upon his approval of the English version. Paz, who had been translated by Ruykeyser and published by Grove Press, found Randall's translation amateurish. Shortly before number 18 went to press he withdrew all but one poem. In a letter to Mondragón he explained that texts written in Spanish very often appeared to be poor translations from the English. Paz said that he was not a purist and, therefore, not easily shocked by Anglicisms and Gallicisms. He did not believe in a pure Spanish. He clarified, however, that writing in living Spanish—while being in constant communication with English, Nahuatl, or Chinese—is one thing and confusing the original act of writing with that of translation is quite another.[63]

Mondragón also published "concrete poetry" from Brazil, new Uruguayan and Guatemalan works, and revolutionary poems from Cuba. At a minimum, his efforts had to persuade attentive American readers that poetry was very much alive in Latin America. His editorship was an excellent attempt to strike a balance between tradition and experimentation. More than his wife, he conceived of the magazine as literary, and he usually avoided extrapoetic digressions. Ironically it was Randall, brought up in a less politicized culture, who embraced social-protest writing and changed the magazine's direction in a way that finally led to its demise.

IV

From the outset the magazine had been influenced by the political uproar of the sixties, but that did not preclude pluralism. Support for
Cuba and opposition to the Vietnam War had mingled with mysticism,
as in this statement of Randall's in 1964: "Any change must begin
within you (me) . . . a single brush hue can do more for man . . .
than all the socially-morally conscious art."[64]

This stance was difficult to sustain. In the overheated atmosphere of
the sixties Randall and Mondragón drew fire from both sides as the
magazine was accused both of backing the left and avoiding political
commitment. The editors' balancing act failed when consensus among
them broke down in late 1965. What brought things to a head was Randall's steady move toward Marxism and Mondragón's growing involvement with the occult. By January 1966 the rift was evident. The
cover of number 17 portrayed Marines disembarking in Santo Domingo
in the famed invasion of 1965. The editors' notes showed their division
even better. While Mondragón stuck to his esoteric ruminations, Randall's note called for increasing militancy: "In the states [*sic*] we saw
what is happening . . . [we] know it cannot be much longer before the
chains give away, the left organizes."[65] Number 18 opened with Picas-
so's "Guernica," a call to end the Vietnam War, and a tribute to the
Colombian guerrilla priest Camilo Torres.

In this new phase, Randall adopted a hard-line editorial stance, which
gradually dominated the whole magazine. Earlier pacifist rhetoric was
replaced by leftist slogans, and tolerance by outright exclusion of dissi-
dent voices. As a reader observed: "Unless you print dissenting opinion
. . . you aren't conducting a search for truth, you are just running a
vehicle for propaganda."[66] The new policy also resulted in stronger ties
with the New Left in the United States and with Cuban and Marxist
groups in Latin America. At this time Randall began exchanges with
publications like *Guerrilla* in Detroit and *Dialog* in New York. The editor of *Guerrilla*, Allen van Newkirk, would regularly report on the
"state of insurrection" in sixties America. A glance at his letter to Randall, published in number 24, shows how far some activists had moved
from the days when they described a civil rights march as an "actual diffusion of love":[67]

This must be understood; that here in Detroit the riots were not race riots. . . . The class basis of the insurrection became apparent, acute here in

Detroit. Anti-white feeling was immediately transformed into ANTI-PROP-ERTY. (THE IMMENSE SCALE OF THE LOOTING AND SYSTEMATIC BURNING OF THE STORES AFTER THEY WERE LOOTED) [*sic*]. This was a dual and combined process.[68]

At the heart of Randall's new policy was extensive coverage of Cuba. In 1963 the magazine had published seven Cuban poets and Castro's "Words to the Intellectuals" but had not been overtly militant. In 1967 the editors traveled to Havana to participate in the "Encuentro con Ruben Darío," which gathered poets from all over the world. Much more than Mondragón, who disapproved of Cuban censorship of the arts, Randall was enchanted with Castro's regime. She willingly became a spokesman for Cuba before American and Latin American members of the little magazine circuit. She established links between American writers and Cuba's publishing house "Casa de las Américas." On the personal level she wrote to friends describing how Cuba had "changed" her life. Poets like Bly, who had little in common with *The Plumed Horn* on literary grounds, eagerly read her accounts and regarded the magazine as a bridge between the United States and the island. Only a handful of Randall's correspondents seemed reluctant to share her excitement. John Brushwood, a professor of Spanish at the University of Missouri, and a friend and collaborator, complained that Randall's letters indicated that she had been brainwashed because she failed to admit Castro was a dictator.[69]

Criticism like this did not stop her from transforming the magazine into a mouthpiece for Castro's government or, as she put it, a challenge to the "U.S. imposed blockade" against Cuba. Number 22 opened with lengthy praise of Castro's cultural policy. The following issue paid homage to the 26th of July, the anniversary of the Cuban revolution. It presented Cuban poetry by Nicolás Guillén, Fayad Jamís, and others— and accounts of the editors' experience in Havana. It is interesting to compare Randall's idyllic view of the island ("Cuba happens to be the only country on the continent to have completely eradicated illiteracy . . . where misery has been stamped out")[70] with the opinions the young Cuban writer José Mario, then living in Havana, expressed to her husband: "Y la situación actual de Cuba, la falta de libertad y las represiones mas ridículas en nombre de la revolución . . . se ha llegado con la juventud a un grado de inhumanidad repugnante." [Consider the situation of Cuba, the lack of freedom and the most absurd repression,

all in the name of the revolution . . . the treatment of the young people has reached a point of loathsome inhumanity.][71]

Randall's commitment to Cuba is most evident in her July 1967 article "Cuba: Impressions from Eight Years of Triumph." This essay,
written in repetitious, pseudo-lyrical prose, viewed the revolution in existential terms: "In cuba [*sic*] the most profound single confrontation is
the change inside a people . . . you must cleanse yourself of press and
preconception in order to come clean to the reality of cuba today."[72] In
contrast to what she deemed the "fallen" state of non-communist countries, she celebrated the purity and fertility of the island: "Cuba is heat.
Cuba is a profusion of palm trees from arrival to departure. . . . Cuba
is rich earth fit for growing everything. And Cuba is people: tough,
joyous, proud, open . . . filled with sun and son."[73] The interviewees
quoted later in the article echo Randall's sentimental view, which went
so far as to justify rationing on the grounds that it was not "deprivation
but rather an aid to filling one's life with other than material values."[74]

Randall also contributed essays on Cuba to *Evergreen* and *Caterpillar*,
then edited by Eshelman. The article she wrote for *Caterpillar* bore the
revealing title "The Answer" and appeared in October, 1967. It focused
on the sexual mores of revolutionary Cuba and was meant to catch the
mood of young intellectuals who found the psychologist William Reich's advocacy of total sexual freedom appealing. According to Reich,
political and sexual revolutions were closely intertwined. Randall
thought she had found the Reichian utopia fulfilled in Cuba: "In Cuba
salaries have nothing to do with sex; and sex is everywhere . . . sex in
Cuba is sex."[75] A confirmed Reichian himself, Eshelman rebuked her
disjointed assumptions. He wrote that he did not believe that Randall
really understood what was happening sexually in Cuba and that she
was smudging this over because she wanted to say something positive
about Cuba.[76]

By 1968 the gap between the editors had become unbridgeable.
Shortly before Mondragón traveled to the United States to be a visiting
professor at a university in Illinois, Randall asked him to move out of
their house and deprived him of veto power in the magazine. Randall
had vocally condemned the Mexican government's repression of student
demonstrations in 1968 and disagreed with her husband's less militant
response to the incident. When Mondragón left the magazine, the Mexican government also withdrew its financial support. Randall had to resort to friends to bring out the next issues.

With Mondragón's departure, the last vestiges of literature for literature's sake vanished. Number 29 was edited solely by Randall and featured revolutionary poetry from Latin America—Guatemalan Otto René Castillo and Peruvian Javier Heraud—and some of Levertov's antiwar poems. The last two issues ever to appear, 30 and 31, were co-edited by Randall and an American, Robert Cohen, her new companion; they lived up to her dictum that literature without a radical political message is worthless. The "Cuban Letters" by a member of Students for a Democratic Society, Michelle Clark, provided the leading piece in the issue. The last number was more doctrinaire in its approach and carried Karl Marx's philosophy in a serious comic strip. At that point Randall also announced that she planned to analyze the content of American media messages and to denounce their bourgeois ideology. The project bore the name of "demystification self-analysis reality feedback" and clearly suggested that as an inter-American literary journal *The Plumed Horn* was dead.

The publication of Randall and Cohen's magazine ended abruptly when the Mexican government ordered their arrest for their involvement in the student movement. In June, 1969 they went into hiding for two months and then left for Cuba. Randall, Cohen, and her four children settled in Havana, where Randall worked as a researcher and writer for the Editorial de Ciencias Sociales of the Instituto Cubano del Libro.

Randall traveled to Chile in 1972 to get a firsthand view of Allende's socialist experiment. In 1980 she visited Nicaragua and wrote *Sandino's Daughters: Testimonies of Nicaraguan Women in Struggle* (1981), a book on the role of women in the Sandinista regime.[77]

In 1984 she returned to the United States and later married an American. Believing she had lost her American citizenship when she became a Mexican national in 1967, she applied for permanent resident status. The Immigration and Naturalization Service denied her application and began deportation proceedings. An immigration judge in El Paso ordered Randall to be deported as an alien who had written and published material advocating "the doctrines of world communism." He based his ruling on the McCarran-Walter Act of 1952 that permits banning foreigners from entering the United States because of their ideological beliefs. After a long legal battle, which caused quite a stir and drew the support of many writers and liberal intellectuals, Randall won her case. The Board of Immigration Appeals ruled in July 1989 that she had never lost her U.S. citizenship and consequently had never legally been subject to deportation.

Randall now lives in Albuquerque, New Mexico and still reviews and writes poetry. As for Mondragón, he remained in Mexico City after the divorce. He continues writing poetry and edits two cultural magazines—one for a Buddhist institute and one for the Union of State Employees (ISSSTE).

The Plumed Horn shared many of the shortcomings of other sixties "littles." In its commitment to the new, early liberalism, and later dogmatism, it often disregarded quality and furnished its readers little guidance concerning standards of taste and thought. Yet, for all its flaws, it exposed American poets to Latin American poetry, in particular new works by young writers. Later in the seventies, magazines like *Road Apple Review* and *The American Poetry Review* and small presses like Dave Oliphant's Prickly Pear Press in Fort Worth have followed Randall and Mondragón's lead in publishing translations of works by Latin American poets. More recently, Curbstone Press in Willimantic, Connecticut has been publishing Latin poets, preferably left-leaning, like the late Salvadoran Roque Dalton and Ernesto Cardenal, whose *Cosmic Canticle* appeared in 1993.

Furthermore, *The Plumed Horn* introduced American intellectuals and artists to such Latin American poets as Cardenal, Pizarnik, and Lihn who later were claimed by New Directions and other New York publishers. In Latin America it created an informed poetic community that in many ways overcame hemispheric borders and cultural isolation. Had the magazine stuck to its original commitment to pluralism, it might have provided an effective model for a lasting inter-American literary exchange. As things turned out, it was the Center of Inter-American Relations that successfully fashioned the dynamic hemispheric literary exchange Randall and Mondragón had pioneered.

NOTES

1. Margaret Randall, "El Corno Emplumado, 1961–1969: Some Notes in Retrospect, 1975," *TriQuarterly* 43 (fall 1978), 407.

2. See *Kulchur* 2 (1960), 19.

3. Randall, *"El Corno Emplumado,"* 407.

4. Ibid.

5. Gilbert Sorrentimo, "Neon Kulchur, ETC," *TriQuarterly* 43 (fall 1978), 300.

6. Editors' Note, *El Corno Emplumado/The Plumed Horn* 1 (January 1962), 5.

7. Robert Cuadra and Edwin Yllescas to Sergio Mondragón, 29 November 1962. All quoted correspondence in this chapter is from the *El Corno Emplumado* Collection in the Harry Ransom Humanities Research Center, The University of Texas at Austin.

8. Clayton Eshelman to Margaret Randall, 17 August 1962.

9. Morris Dickstein, *Gates of Eden* (New York: Basic Books, 1977), 58.

10. See Rita Guibert's *Seven Voices* (New York: Alfred A. Knopf, 1973), 373.

11. Norman Mailer, quoted in Dennis Wrong, "The American Left and Cuba," *Commentary* (February 1962), 100.

12. Ibid., 103.

13. Robert Bly, "What if after so many wings of birds," *Neruda and Vallejo* (Boston: Beacon Press, 1971), 172.

14. Robert Bly, "The Surprise of Neruda," *The Sixties* 7 (winter 1964), 19.

15. Bly, "What if after," 174.

16. Kirby Congdon to Margaret Randall, 24 March 1963.

17. Clayton Eshelman, Typescript, *El Corno Emplumado* Collection, HRHRC, UT, Austin.

18. Margaret Randall, "Thoughts on the Poetic Line, Where We Are Now, Collective," *Kulchur* 18 (June 1965), 26.

19. Ibid., 27.

20. Margaret Randall, "An Epic with Meaning for Now," *Trace* 50 (autumn 1963), 254–56.

21. Cid Corman to Margaret Randall, 31 March 1966.

22. Margaret Randall, "Letter to the Editor," *Trace* (1967), 330.

23. Margaret Randall, "Letter to the Editor," *Trace* (spring 1963), 13.

24. Thomas Merton to Margaret Randall, "Letter," *El Corno Emplumado* 23 (July 1967), 160.

25. Thomas Merton, "Letter," *El Corno Emplumado* 6 (April 1963), 163.

26. Thomas Merton to Margaret Randall, 9 October 1963.

27. Ibid.

28. Lawrence Ferlinghetti to Margaret Randall, 27 April 1964.

29. See Jane Kramer, *Allen Ginsberg in America* (New York: Random House, 1969).

30. Allen Ginsberg to Margaret Randall, 10 March 1962.

31. Lawrence Ferlinghetti, "A Tirade for C. W. Mills," *El Corno Emplumado* 5 (January 1963), 117.

32. Robert Kelly to Margaret Randall, 19 July 1963.

33. Robert Kelly to Margaret Randall, 10 December 1965.

34. Paul Blackburn, "The International Word," *Nation*, 21 April 1962, 358.

35. Paul Blackburn to Margaret Randall, 13 May 1962.

36. Ed Dorn to Margaret Randall, no date, 1966.

37. Ed Dorn to Margaret Randall, 26 October 1966.

38. Ed Dorn to Margaret Randall, 22 November 1967.

39. Margaret Randall, "Thoughts on the Poetic Line, where we are now, collective," *Kulchur* 18 (June 1965), 26.

40. Denise Levertov to Margaret Randall, 6 October 1966.

41. Ted Enslin, "Letter to the Editors," *El Corno Emplumado* 19 (July 1966), 184.

42. Denise Levertov, "Letter to the Editors," *El Corno Emplumado* 21 (January 1967), 131.

43. Ibid., 132.

44. Robert Bly to Margaret Randall, 24 April 1962.

45. Clayton Eshelman to Margaret Randall, 3 May 1965.

46. Editors' Note, *El Corno Emplumado* 3 (July 1962), 5.

47. Carol Berge to Margaret Randall, 24 April (exact year not available).

48. Dickstein, *Gates of Eden*, 275.

49. Carol Berge, "Letter to the Editors," *El Corno Emplumado* 5 (January 1963), 151.

50. Ted Enslin to Margaret Randall, no date.

51. Eleanor Antin to Margaret Randall, 15 September 1966.

52. Ernesto Cardenal to Sergio Mondragón, 20 May 1962.

53. Ernesto Cardenal to Sergio Mondragón, no date.

54. Ernesto Cardenal to Sergio Mondragón, 1 December 1963.

55. Ibid.

56. Nota de los Editores, *El Corno Emplumado* 13 (January 1965), 5.

57. Eduardo Garavaglia to Sergio Mondragón, no date.

58. Alexandra Pizarnik to Sergio Mondragón, 4 April 1965.

59. "Manifesto Nadaista al Homo Sapiens," Typescript, *El Corno Emplumado* Collection, HRHRC, UT, Austin.

60. Gonzalo Arango to Sergio Mondragón, no date.

61. Walter Loewenfels, "Report on *AJY TOJEN*," Typescript, *El Corno Emplumado* Collection, HRHRC, UT, Austin.

62. Clayton Eshelman to Sergio Mondragón and Margaret Randall, 12 January 1966.

63. Octavio Paz to Sergio Mondragón, 19 February 1966.

64. Editors' Note, *El Corno Emplumado* 11 (July 1964), 5.

65. Editor's Note, *El Corno Emplumado* 17 (January 1966), 6.

66. Seymour Faust to Margaret Randall, 21 September 1966.

67. Alex and Meredith, "Letter to Editors," *El Corno Emplumado* 9 (January 1964), 147.

68. Allen van Newkirk, "Letters to Editors," *El Corno Emplumado* 24 (October 1967), 163.

69. John Brushwood to Margaret Randall, 25 June 1967.

70. Editors' Note, *El Corno Emplumado* 23 (July 1967), 6.

71. José Mario to Sergio Mondragón, 11 October 1964.

72. Margaret Randall, "Cuba: Impressions from Eight Years of Triumph," *El Corno Emplumado* 23 (July 1967), 138.

73. Ibid., 139.

74. Ibid., 143.

75. Margaret Randall, Typescript, *El Corno Emplumado* Collection, HRHRC, UT, Austin.

76. Clayton Eshelman to Margaret Randall, no date.

77. For an account of Randall's conversion of Castro to communism, see Margaret Randall, *Part of the Solution/Portrait of a Revolutionary* (New York: New Directions, 1973).

Casa de las Américas and the Center for Inter-American Relations: Competing for Latin American Literature

It was not until the late sixties that Latin American literature began to make a significant mark on the U.S. cultural scene. Given the aggressive support of Latin American authors by Casa de las Américas and the rising popularity of modern Latin American fiction in Europe at the time, champions of Hispanic and Brazilian culture, grouped around the Center for Inter-American Relations in New York, decided it was time for this country to catch up.

The center was established in 1967 by David Rockefeller, then president of the Chase Manhattan Bank. Aware that earlier attempts to introduce Latin American letters had had only a limited impact, he wanted the organization to be a vehicle for a closer and continuing rapport with the United States' southern neighbors. To this end the center's literature program strove to gain a reputation among mainstream critics and publishers for Latin American writers. Over a period of fifteen years the center worked as a clearinghouse for Latin writing. It subsidized translations, stirred up enthusiasm for novelists and poets among publishers and reviewers from prominent New York publications and provided an outlet where Latin American culture could be discussed.

I

Unlike poets, who incorporated into their work European avant-garde ideas during the twenties and thirties, Latin American novelists, with some exceptions, were slower in assimilating modernism. When they finally did, however, they radically changed the course of Ibero-American letters. In the early sixties South America witnessed an outburst of experimental fiction that came to be known as the "boom" of the Latin American novel. It was unique in more than a purely literary sense. For the first time a generation of innovators succeeded in capturing both local and international attention.

The most visible figures associated with the boom were Mexican Carlos Fuentes, Colombian Gabriel García Márquez, Peruvian Mario Vargas Llosa, Argentine Julio Cortázar, Chilean José Donoso and Cuban Guillermo Cabrera Infante. The first four writers named appear in all the accounts of boom membership; the other three and such younger novelists as Cuban Severo Sarduy, Argentine Manuel Puig and Cuban José Lezama Lima are sometimes included.

The boom novelists certainly enriched the art of writing fiction in Latin America. They redirected fictional concerns from the realistic depiction of social life to an overwhelming preoccupation with language, fantasy, and artifice. They exploited the technical innovations of such modernists as William Faulkner, John Dos Passos, and James Joyce, while at the same time making fantasy an important ingredient of their work.[1] But technical exuberance is not what set them apart from their predecessors. In fact, their works are in a direct line of succession from those authors who in the late thirties and forties challenged the premises of the naturalistic-regionalistic novel and initiated the renovation of the genre. Faced with the problem of finding less constricting forms of expression, writers like Borges, Roberto Arlt, and Ernesto Sábato in Argentina; Miguel Angel Asturias in Guatemala; Alejo Carpentier in Cuba; Juan Rulfo and Agustín Yañez in Mexico; María Luisa Bombal in Chile; and Juan Carlos Onetti in Uruguay played with linear time and delved into fantasy or planted the seeds of magic realism that García Márquez would carry to fame in the late sixties.

The boom writers' crucial contribution was more than merely aesthetic. An outstanding feature of the boom coterie was its sense of importance as a group of innovators and their determination to be recognized in Europe and the United States. What seems to have been most disturbing to them was the almost total obscurity in which their brilliant forerunners had worked. Unlike Borges, they resisted the idea of enjoying a merely national reputation. Estranged from their local literary establishments, they envisioned a cosmopolitan destiny for themselves. And, as José Donoso observes, this was new: "Before 1960 it was very uncommon to hear laymen speak of the 'contemporary Spanish American novel': there were Uruguayan or Ecuadorian, Mexican or Venezuelan novels. The novels of each country were confined within that country's own frontiers and the novel's fame and relevance [was] a local affair. . . . The novelist in the Spanish American countries wrote for his parish: about the problems of his parish and in the language of his parish."[2]

Nowhere was their sense of being noteworthy more evident than in their definition of their aesthetic allegiances. Nearly all the members of the boom circle attempted to rewrite the history of Latin American fiction and define the boundaries of what they called "la nueva novela" [the new novel]. A case in point is Vargas Llosa's essay "Primitives and Creators." He referred to novelists of the first half of the century, such as Mariano Azuela and Rómulo Gallegos, as "primitives" and quickly dismissed them: "In this picturesque and rural novel the countryside predominates over the city, the landscape over the character. . . . The technique is rudimentary, pre-Flaubertian. . . ."[3] To the "primitives" he opposed a generation of "creators," among which he places Borges, Onetti, himself, and fellow boom members. Their distinctive mark, he maintained, is their experimental vocation and diversity.

While the Peruvian measured the gap between regionalism and modernism in terms of movement away from the local and the didactic, Fuentes saw it a different way. In probably the most eloquent interpretation of the "nueva novela," he criticized the artistic and social bankruptcy of the regionalists: "La novela tradicional de América Latina aparece como una forma estática dentro de una sociedad estática. . . . La novela está capturada en las redes de la realidad inmediata y sólo puede reflejarla." [The traditional Latin American novel is a static form within a static society. . . . The novel is trapped by immediate reality and can only reflect it.][4]

Between the regionalists and his generation, Fuentes drew a sharp dividing line. The regionalists never wrote novels, he said—mere anachronistic sketches. Fuentes viewed his generation's achievements in almost heroic terms. Not only did they write the first Latin American novel, he argued, but they understood their culture in its full complexity:

[Las] novelas poseen la fuerza de enfrentar la realidad latinoamericana, pero no ya como un hecho regional, sino como parte de una vida que afecta a todos los hombres, . . . no es definible con sencillez maniquea, sino que revela un movimiento de conflictos ambiguos.

[The novels have the strength to confront Latin American reality, not as a regional phenomenon but as part of a life which affects all men. It is not characterized by Manichean simplicity, but by a movement of ambiguous conflicts.][5]

Fuentes was the first to locate the importance of the boom novel on precisely aesthetic grounds. Like a narrative of Faulkner or Joyce, the boom novel, he emphasized, is above all a feat of language. Fuentes's claim was amplified by the foremost boom critic, Uruguayan Emir Rodríguez Monegal, and the numerous scholars under his influence.[6]

In a more sociological assessment, José Donoso explained his generation's distinctiveness in terms of its exposure to wider ranges of influence than its ancestors. As a result the boom novel acquired a cosmopolitan and cross-cultural orientation that facilitated its acceptance outside Latin America.[7]

What is important is not the truth or falsehood of these statements, but the debate they kindled throughout the region, surely one of the liveliest in the history of Latin American letters. Though Fuentes and other apologists acknowledged their debt to earlier experimenters, chiefly Borges, boom detractors saw in their statements pride, plain snobbery, and even ignorance. One of the boldest boom denouncers was Cuban critic Manuel Pedro González, who contended there was little new in the "nueva novela." It was just warmed over modernism, its technical pirouettes poor derivations of Joyce, Proust, and Faulkner. The boom clique, he warned, had taken the wrong path to fame: "Por el descarriladero del mimetismo y la contrahechura de modelos extranjeros, la narrativa hispanoamericana jamás alcanzará jerarquía. Por esos vericuetos se desemboca en el colonialismo artístico y mental." [By running on the track of mimesis and counterfeit foreign models, Latin American fiction will never gain recognition. Following those rugged paths only leads to artistic and mental colonialism.][8] Less adamant was critic Fernando Alegría, who insisted the boom was not a revolution but a logical evolution of the hemisphere's tradition of experiment.[9]

The loudest boom defamers were those who saw it as a "political commercial clique" rather than a literary movement. Argentine José Blanco Amor thought the whole thing a media event and went so far as to deny the significance of writers like Fuentes or Cortázar. In a series of articles published by the Buenos Aires newspaper *La Prensa* in 1976 and entitled "El Final del Boom," he assaulted the boom writers' often declared concern for hemispheric problems: "América Latina es un pretexto: ellos escriben para informar a Europa y a sus amigos europeos acerca de la situación de la literatura en esta parte del mundo." [Latin

America is just a pretext. They write to inform Europe and their European friends about literature in this part of the world.][10]

The fact that boom novelists deliberately played off one another— García Márquez alludes to Fuentes's *Artemio Cruz* and Cortázar's *Hopscotch* in *One Hundred Years of Solitude* —fueled the arguments of those who resented the clubbish nature of the boom. In their eyes, the boom was a mutual admiration society that deftly promoted itself in Paris, Barcelona, and Mexico City. The detractors also objected to the boom writers' politics. Critics on the right called attention to the boom authors' Cuban links and their often half-baked denunciation of American imperialism. The Left accused them of having succumbed to the temptations of capitalism—juicy royalties and stardom. Chilean critic Hernán Vidal and Uruguayan Marxist scholar Angel Rama summarized this point of view: "Este vedetismo funciona al servicio del sistema. No se trata del prestigio artístico, ni de la conducción espiritual o ideológica o artística de una sociedad, sino de la servidumbre a sus mecanismos de publicidad." [This stardom serves the system. It is not a question of artistic prestige or the spiritual, ideological, or artistic direction of society, but of becoming a slave to publicity.][11]

Predictably, all this criticism magnified the boom. By the late sixties in Latin America the boom novelists were almost mythical figures, perceived as sophisticated and powerful manipulators of the European and American literary scenes. Outside the region their backers added to the legend by maintaining that the boom had brought back to life a dying genre. As New York writer Sarah Crichton put it: "Here [in the United States], with our novels of suburban custom and marital intrigue, words often seem to have the potency of a blow dryer on a windmill. There [in Latin America], words still have real power."[12]

Now that the frenzy has cooled down, one can better assess the real importance of the boom. The writers' contention that the "nueva novela" was original because it was above all a feat of language needs to be readjusted. As critic Raymond Williams has asserted, the boom novelists' modernist project, unlike that of their U.S. and European counterparts, never quite lost sight of its underlying political and cultural grounding: "[They] still believed, through the 1960s, in the possibility of articulating truths, although they adopted many of the narrative strategies pioneered by First World modernists."[13]

Though in a way one can agree with Angel Rama's economic perception of the boom (i.e., that it was partly the product of marketing), its accomplishments cannot be overlooked.[14] For the first time Latin

American novelists overcame their isolation and became aware of one another. At the same time they made the world aware of them. "La nueva novela," a blend of literary modernism and a concern with Latin American history and identity, was undoubtedly appealing to international publishers in the mid-sixties. A good deal of the infatuation with leftist ideology during this era originated in Castro's revolutionary Cuba, which gave the boom writers their first important international exposure.

II

Before it became overtly Stalinist, Castro's socialism captured the fancy of a large number of Latin American artists and intellectuals. Association with Cuba, as Donoso observed, was a major element in the rise of Spanish American fiction to international fame: "I think that . . . political unanimity—or near unanimity—. . .[provided] an ideological structure to which one could be more or less close . . . and for a time [gave] the feeling of continental [i.e., Latin American] cohesion."[15]

To understand the exhilaration over the sense of collective identity brought about by Cuba one must look at the situation of young Latin American writers before 1960. They lived isolated from the rest of the continent, not to mention the world, and they had few opportunities to overcome that isolation by being published for a more than national audience. Furthermore, the literary scene in Latin America, insofar as one existed, was dominated by regionalists distrustful of outsiders and experimenters.[16]

It was mainly these two problems that Casa de las Américas in Havana sought to redress. The cultural institution was founded in 1960. Profiting from the worldwide attention Cuba enjoyed after the revolution, its director Haydée Santa María made the dissemination of "new" Latin American writing a top priority and succeeded in her mission. Cuba's "cultural revolution" broke down the geographical barriers that had kept writers apart by making each local literature a more than national affair. Havana replaced Paris as the intellectual capital of Latin America and became a meeting place for those who envisioned themselves as avant-gardists. Literary experiments were no longer disparaged but placed within the frame of the revolution—to be an experimenter was to be politically progressive. Younger authors were given the opportunity to see their work in print for the first time. Statements like "la cultura latinoamericana se está haciendo en Cuba desde Casa de las

Américas" [Latin American culture is being made in Cuba from Casa de las Américas][17] contained a great deal of truth for emerging novelists like Vargas Llosa and Fuentes.

Throughout the sixties Casa de las Américas extended generous invitations to Latin American writers and intellectuals. A conscious agent of the "Cubanization" of Latin American culture was the poet and later director of Casa de las Américas, Roberto Fernández Retamar. Fernández had been a professor of Spanish at Yale. He was well read, spoke several languages, and in his frequent trips to Mexico impressed members of the Fuentes's clique with his refinement.[18] As a result of his endeavors, many of those who had met him in Mexico ended up in Havana at one time or another during the early sixties. In Cuba the guests of the regime participated in well-publicized literary political colloquia that provided the opportunity to discuss their work and meet celebrities like Susan Sontag and Françoise Sagan, both at the time faithful worshippers of Castro. Though these gatherings had a carnival and propagandist tone, they furnished writers with much needed contacts and stimuli.

Memorable among the Havana "happenings" was the annual meeting to vote on the then prestigious literary award Premio Casa de las Américas. Members of the boom circle dutifully flocked to Havana and took turns being part of the jury granting the prize. In 1960 Carlos Fuentes presided over the jury, his presence surrounded by publicity. He participated in "dialogues" with Cuban novelists Carpentier and Cabrera Infante that were broadcast on national television. He also led a panel discussion on a favorite topic, "La Revolución Cubana y Nuestra América."[19] In 1961 it was Asturias's turn to be on the jury. Cortázar followed him in 1962. Vargas Llosa did his stint as judge in 1965 and enthusiastically partook of the fanfare surrounding the "premio." He had to submit to hearing his novel *The Time of the Hero* (1962) being lavishly praised in a round-table discussion at the headquarters of Casa de las Américas.[20]

The most important contribution of Cuba's cultural institution was its *Revista Casa de las Américas*, a literary and cultural quarterly that brought together many Latin authors. Its original editors, poets Fausto Maso and Antón Arrufat, encouraged experiment and innovation in writing. During the early sixties this liberal editorial policy turned the journal into the most important outlet for the younger generation of Latin American authors. Fuentes's as yet unabated enthusiasm for Castro made him a regular contributor. His belief that literature and revolution

were inseparable explain the political bent of the essays he submitted to
Revista. "Radiografía de los Estados Unidos," published in 1961, exam-
ined the issue of American imperial designs in Latin America. The
magazine also issued a wide range of his literary work. In 1960 it carried a chapter of his novel *La patria de nadie.* His short story "Cholula"
appeared in the fall issue of 1964 and an excerpt of his novel *A Change
of Skin* in 1967. Cortázar was equally devoted to *Revista.* During the
sixties he visited Cuba regularly and contributed to the journal samples
of his work. A chapter of the novel *Rayuela* was featured in the October
1964 issue. In 1967 the short story "Me cargo y me levanto" was
printed. His political concerns also found a niche in the magazine. The
last issue of 1967 carried his open letter to the current editor, Fernández
Retamar. There he lyrically outlined the possibilities that Cuban cultural policies had made available to Latin American intellectuals:

El contacto personal con las realizaciones de la revolución, la amistad y el
diálogo con escritores y artistas, lo positivo y lo negativo que vi . . . actu-
aron doblemente en mi; por un lado tocaba otra vez la realidad latinoamericana de la que tan alejado me había sentido en el terreno personal, y por otro
lado asistía cotidianamente a la dura y a veces desesperada tarea de edificar el
socialismo. . . . Sin razonarlo, sin análisis previo, viví de pronto el sen-
timiento maravilloso de que mi camino ideológico coincidiera con mi re-
torno latinoamericano.

[Being in touch with the accomplishments of the revolution, befriending
and talking with artists and writers, sensing the negative and the positive,
had a double effect on me. On the one hand I came close to Latin American
reality, which I had felt so alien for a long time; on the other, I participated
in the harsh and often desperate task of building socialism. . . . Without
reasoning and without previous analysis I realized that my ideological quest
coincided with my return to Latin America.][21]

Even more directly involved was Vargas Llosa. During the early sixties he was a member of the editorial board of *Revista.* Excerpts from
his novels and short stories, like "Pichula Cuéllar," as well as critical
articles appeared regularly in the journal. Other authors linked to *Revista* included Donoso, Sábato, and Asturias.

Casa de las Américas also filled a vacuum in the area of literary criticism. With the exception of *Sur* and *Marcha* in Montevideo, most critical journals in Latin America had disappeared and been inadequately replaced by literary supplements of big newspapers, such as *Siempre* in
Mexico City. Thus *Revista* and the Centro de Investigaciones Literarias

of the Casa de las Américas became important sources for understanding the boom novels. Throughout the decade they published collections of critical essays devoted to García Márquez, Onetti, Lezama Lima, and others. Notwithstanding the fact that the point of view of these essays became increasingly political as the decade progressed, they were forerunners in the study of the new literature.

The unity of Latin intellectuals cultivated by Havana was suddenly shattered when the Padilla case exploded in 1971. Three years earlier, when Cuban poet Heberto Padilla had won a prize awarded by the U.N.E.A.C. (Cuban Writers and Artists' League), he had run into trouble with the regime for the allegedly "counterrevolutionary" content of his work, *Fuera del juego* (1969). He was imprisoned and forced to undergo "self-criticism" (i.e., public confession). As Cabrera Infante explained the episode to English-speaking readers: "Now we had a public confession that was quite a show. Padilla, not reading from any script but obviously following a scenario in a very Orthodox Russian and un-Cuban Catholic way, confessed to all kinds of literary and political crimes, and even crimes against the state and people of Cuba."[22]

Padilla's detention was part of a series of attempts to curtail cultural freedom in Cuba, the first of which occurred in 1962. The regime had then closed down the avant-garde publication *Lunes de Revolución* and forced its editor, Cabrera Infante, into exile. At the time Cabrera's plight was either ignored or dismissed as a case of bureaucratic harassment or personality conflicts—in any case a trivial matter. Cabrera's denunciations of Castro's repressive policies printed by the Argentine weekly *Primera Plana* in 1968 came under heavy attack from many Latin authors who still perceived the island as a model of cultural vitality.

The Padilla case dealt a heavy blow to Havana's standing among Latin American writers. With very few exceptions, most authors supported their colleague. Many realized that Padilla's troubles were caused by the displacement of cultural open-mindedness by orthodox Marxism. Publishing standards were ruled by Castro's dictum: "Within the revolution everything / against the revolution nothing." The artists' union had become a branch of the Communist party in the late sixties and books suspected of "reactionary" messages were ordered off the shelves. But it was in *Revista* that Castro's crackdown was most noticeable. In 1965 the liberal Arrufat was removed from his editorial position for having invited Allen Ginsberg to Cuba. The poet had boisterously condemned Castro's persecution of homosexuals. Arrufat was replaced by the orthodox Fernández Retamar whose editorship explicitly emphasized politics over literature.

The first authors to abandon the Cuban cause were Fuentes and Vargas Llosa. Of the two, the Peruvian became the most vocal critic of Castro. He repeatedly stated that the "loss of freedom is too high a price to pay. Freedom is an ingredient of justice, so you cannot sacrifice freedom to achieve justice."[23] Many followed his lead and ceased collaboration with the journal or dealings with Havana at all. Thus the spirit of cohesion dissolved. The Padilla case separated Latin American intellectuals into antagonistic camps. The long friendship between Vargas Llosa and García Márquez came to an end. At the same time that Vargas Llosa broke with Havana, both Cortázar and García Márquez chose to refrain from overt criticism of Castro's regime. Later on they became fervent propagandists of Cuba and frequently visited the island to lend their prestige to Castro's policies. An indication of Castro's appreciation of their support, several observers asserted, was the fact that both writers were allowed a degree of freedom in *Revista* that was denied Cuban authors.

Despite the sour ending, the close connection between Cuba and Latin American intellectuals brought many mutual gains while it lasted. Taking advantage of a Latin American cultural tradition that makes intellectuals the moral conscience of nations, Casa de las Américas mobilized their talent and used their prestige to promote the image of a progressive, humanitarian revolution. The writers, in turn, benefited from the world attention bestowed on Castro's regime throughout the decade.

III

The euphoria of Cuba's cultural revolution spread throughout the hemisphere. Influential magazines like *Marcha* in Montevideo and *Siempre* in Mexico City and avant-garde publishers like Jorge Alvarez in Buenos Aires eagerly followed the ferment of ideas and publicity that burgeoned in Havana. Cuba also influenced government initiatives in Latin America. The most notable was the establishment of the Rómulo Gallegos Award, which the Venezuelan Instituto Nacional de la Cultura presents every five years to a Latin American novelist for a distinguished book. In 1967 it went to Vargas Llosa for *La casa verde* (1966) and in 1972 to García Márquez for *One Hundred Years of Solitude* (1967). Of all literary programs modeled after Havana, the Venezuelan one, according to

Rodríguez Monegal, was the least political since it did not require that writers pass a leftist or rightist litmus test.[24]

Cuban influence was also partly responsible for finding an audience for Latin American writing outside the region. Few publishers benefited more than Carlos Barral of the firm Seix Barral in Barcelona. A poet and an avowed socialist, Barral traveled to Cuba during the sixties and befriended many of the members of the boom clique. These connections served him well. In 1961 Seix Barral initiated a steady production of Latin fiction that continued well into the seventies. Carlos Barral also helped establish the Premio Biblioteca Breve, which for the most part was granted to authors linked to the "nueva novela." Vargas Llosa's *La ciudad y los perros* received it in 1962 and Fuentes's *Cambio de piel* in 1967. The Barral-Latin American network prompted much criticism in Spanish and Latin intellectual circles. Allegations revolved around the composition of the jury for the Biblioteca Breve prize. Vargas Llosa and García Márquez presented prizes to fellow novelists Cabrera Infante and Fuentes, who later returned the favor. Nevertheless, the award and Barral's publishing policies played an important role in introducing Latin American fiction to Europe. Operating from Barcelona, an important cultural center for the Hispanic world, allowed authors to learn the ropes of large-scale European publishing.[25]

It was in Barcelona that the boom writers met the aggressive literary agent Carmen Balcells, who in the late sixties helped bring their works to European and, later, American markets. To this day the representative of many Latin American authors, she is responsible for the healthy contracts García Márquez and Neruda have been able to obtain. A glimpse of her working style and personality can be obtained from a note critic and editor Ronald Christ wrote her after one of her trips to New York: "It has been very warm here since you left. Chiefly I think because we lost the whirlwind you created with your twenty-two appointments every day. I get tired thinking of it."[26]

Outside of Spain, the European country most receptive to Latin American novels was France. Much of the credit goes to Roger Caillois's series "La Croix du Sud." In 1968 its publisher, Gallimard, transferred its Latin American authors to the collection "Du Monde Entier"[27]—a significant step.

Caillois had more success than Alfred A. Knopf and James Laughlin in the United States. Knopf, incidentally, often followed his lead—in whetting the appetite of fellow French publishers. Les Editions du

Seuil, for example, devoted a large portion of its series "Ecrivains Etrangers" to Latin Americans.

The magazine *Mundo Nuevo* was created in 1966 to cater to the new European enthusiasm for Latin American literature. Rodríguez Monegal, former professor of Spanish and Portuguese at Yale, edited the magazine until 1968. As editor of *Marcha* in Uruguay, he had become interested in the boom novel. During the fifties he had corresponded with Carpentier, who sent him his novels *The Lost Steps* and *The Kingdom of This World* to be reviewed in the magazine. At the time he had also befriended Asturias, then Guatemala's ambassador in Buenos Aires and received a copy of *El señor Presidente* (1946). Later in 1962 when he attended the Congreso de Intelectuales held in Concepción, Chile, he met Fuentes and Donoso. Getting to know Fuentes turned out to be crucial for *Mundo Nuevo* and the boom as a whole. It was the Mexican who introduced Rodríguez Monegal to García Márquez in Mexico City and later forwarded to Paris excerpts of *One Hundred Years of Solitude*, then in progress.[28]

The main goal of *Mundo Nuevo* was to place Latin American writing in a wider and more cosmopolitan context. Appropriately, the magazine had its headquarters in Paris. From there Rodríguez Monegal and his associate, Mexican Tomás Segovia, tried to interpret Latin America for Spanish-reading Europeans and relate international issues to the region's literary scene.

Mundo Nuevo was short-lived and prey to the usual Latin political intrigues from the very beginning. This should not obscure the fact, however, that the journal represented some of the best South American writing of the fifties and sixties. Aware of the fact that Latin authors are probably more involved in politics than any other group of writers in the world, the editor designed a format that combined literature with politics and social commentary.

From reading *Mundo Nuevo* one gains a wonderful sense of the richness of the "nueva novela." For many people, the magazine was something of an official organ of the boom, since the writers most closely associated with it were Fuentes, García Márquez, Cabrera Infante, and Severo Sarduy. At the time most of them were living in Europe and undergoing a small-scale Lost Generation experience. To a group that had chosen to view its culture from the outside, the journal provided the perfect outlet. The most striking feature of the publication was its dialogues with Latin authors. In fact, *Mundo Nuevo* began its first issue with an interview with Fuentes in which he discussed the problems of being a writer in Latin America:

America Latina . . . es una especie de Balcanes de la cultura, sobre todo en la vida literaria. Esta llena de Bosnias-Herzegovinas, de terroristas a lo Gavrilo Prinzip. . . . Hay que salir un poco a respirar aire puro, a tomar perspectivas. Creo también que hay cierta tensión en la vida cultural de nuestros paises, la tensión nacida de esa demora a la que se refería Alfonso Reyes cuando decía: "Llegamos siempre con cien años de retraso a los banquetes de la civilización.

[Latin America is a kind of cultural Balkans, especially in its literary life. It is full of Bosnia-Herzegovinas and terrorists Gavrilo Prinzip style. . . . One needs to leave and get some fresh air and new perspectives. I also think that there is tension in the cultural life of our countries, a tension that springs from that lag to which Alfonso Reyes referred when he said: "We always arrive one hundred years late for the banquets of civilization."]²⁹

Other interviews featured Borges, Sábato, and Sarduy, who discussed modern Latin writing against the background of the Parisian critical theories then in vogue.

Mundo Nuevo also offered a wide array of works in progress. Aside from publishing chapters of *One Hundred Years of Solitude* in 1966 and 1967, it carried excerpts from Donoso's *The Obscene Bird of the Night* and Fuentes's *A Change of Skin* in 1968. The same year Cabrera Infante submitted samples of *Three Trapped Tigers*, and Manuel Puig parts of his novel *Betrayed by Rita Hayworth*. The review also displayed lesser-known novelists like Lezama Lima and Guimarães Rosa and such poets as Paz and Peruvian Carlos Germán Belli. Rodríguez Monegal resigned the editorship of *Mundo Nuevo* in 1968 over what he maintained was a disagreement concerning the location of the editorial office of the journal. The editor's abrupt departure, however, was part of a more tangled story that linked the magazine and ILARI, the foundation that funded it, to the *Encounter*-CIA affair disclosed in 1967. The *New York Times* and the magazine *Ramparts* had run a series of articles about CIA connections to intellectuals in which they argued that the British literary journal *Encounter* had received CIA funds by way of the Congress for Cultural Freedom. The American government's justification of this covert funding was to defend pro-Western values in an intellectual milieu perceived as being increasingly dominated by Marxism. The editors of *Encounter*, Stephen Spender and Frank Kermode, who at first denied these accusations, resigned when Melvin Lasky, a member of the editorial board, acknowledged ties to the CIA.[30]

Like *Encounter*, *Mundo Nuevo* had been sponsored by the Latin American branch of the Congress for Cultural Freedom. Though the actual funds came from the Ford Foundation, which had no ties to the CIA, the *Encounter* incident caused the premature ending of the magazine. The disclosures shattered collaborators' confidence and fueled Havana's allegations that the journal was a facade for the CIA. Rodríguez Monegal's ardent defense of his independence was not enough to dispel doubts.[31] The fact that he had been selected by Spender to edit *Mundo Nuevo* and that he had contributed articles on Latin American writing to *Encounter* seemed to prove his complicity. One fact is worth underlining: whatever the source of its funds, the Congress for Cultural Freedom did not dictate editorial policy to the magazines it supported. In the case of *Mundo Nuevo*, it did not hinder criticism of U.S. policies in Vietnam or Latin America.[32]

Though the magazine kept its name after Rodríguez Monegal resigned, everything else changed. The journal was moved to Buenos Aires, where it closed in 1971. The new editors de-emphasized literature in favor of political and sociological topics, at the same time that they welcomed articles that criticized the boom.

Mundo Nuevo appears not to have been widely read in this country. Nonetheless, it represents an important American attempt to support Latin American literature. Understanding the powerful influence Cuba had gained among Latin intellectuals, the Congress for Cultural Freedom apparently saw the magazine as a source of views different from the militant opinions emanating from Casa de las Américas. *Mundo Nuevo*'s concern with the most advanced trends in Latin American writing and its non-partisan editorial outlook account for its popularity among readers throughout the hemisphere.[33]

IV

The most important effort to disseminate modern Latin American literature in the United States was initiated in 1962 by the Inter-American Foundation for the Arts (IAFA) and carried forward by the Center for Inter-American Relations in the late sixties and seventies.

Traditionally drawn to the Left, Latin intellectuals had almost unanimously cheered Castro's coming to power in 1959. They envisioned the Cuban revolution as a positive alternative for Latin America. They were by habit anti-American, and U.S. policies toward Cuba in the early 1960s—lack of diplomatic recognition, economic blockade, and the Bay of Pigs invasion—only intensified this bias. To many important Latin American writers, American policies in the region looked exploitative and shortsighted.

Against this background IAFA was born. The New York–based foundation was established in 1962 by a group of community leaders and businessmen led by Rodman Rockefeller, Nelson Rockefeller's oldest son. Rodman was chairman of the board of the International Basic Economy Corporation, which works jointly with Latin American official and private groups on programs of economic and social development. The Rockefellers' interest in Latin America predates the foundation by several decades. In 1937 Nelson Rockefeller traveled to Venezuela as director of the Creole Petroleum Company, a subsidiary of the family controlled Standard Oil of New Jersey. While in Venezuela Rockefeller bought a ranch and became interested in that country's culture. During World War II Nelson coordinated U.S. relations with its southern neighbors for the Roosevelt administration. Rodman shared his father's passion for Latin American archaeology and art.

Though never overtly stated, the intention behind IAFA was to counteract the impact of Cuba's cultural revolution on Latin intellectuals. IAFA's goal was to show U.S. interest in the art of its alienated neighbors, hoping thus to allay suspicion and rancor. IAFA was a private institution with no visible links to Washington. Despite the fact that its plan fit well with those of the Alliance for Progress, great emphasis was placed on its independence. Members of the board included Edward Albee, William Styron, Lillian Hellman, Gore Vidal, Alfred Knopf, and Argentine filmmaker Leopoldo Torres Nilson, as well as prominent Latin and North American businessmen. Evidently the most conspicuous among these names were those of literary stars. Their presence was meant to revive the inter-American dialogue the Good Neighbor Policy had sparked during World War II—a dialogue that had largely ended in the fifties when American foreign policy focused primarily on Europe and the Far East.

IAFA devoted most of its energy to staging memorable intellectual encounters. With occasional backing from the National Council for the Arts, it organized four inter-American symposia over a period of five years. The first two took place in the Bahamas (1962) and Puerto Rico (1963). The most notable in this series of meetings were the last two held in Chichén Itzá, Mexico (1964), and Puerto Azul, Venezuela (1967).

The Chichén Itzá gathering was organized by IAFA director Robert Wool, a former correspondent for *Look* who had traveled extensively in Latin America. The meeting called to mind a Casa de las Américas "happening" in its display of luminaries and publicity. Among the participants were Styron, Hellman, Knopf, James Laughlin, and anthropologist Oscar Lewis from the United States. The Latin delegation was larger but no less dazzling. It included Fuentes, Rodríguez Monegal, José Donoso, Juan Rulfo, José Luis Cuevas, Nicanor Parra, and Argentine-Colombian art critic Marta Traba. Most of these people had either supported Castro or identified themselves with center leftist political views. Conspicuously absent were conservatives like Borges and fellow Argentines Adolfo Bioy Casares and Victoria Ocampo.

With Mayan ruins in the background, and sumptuous meals and bibulous parties in the foreground, the gathering resembled more a jet set affair than an intellectual convention. The themes proposed for discussion were open-ended and hazy. Among the welter of high-minded topics, such as "Human Problems of Our Cities," only "The Vietnam War" sparked some enthusiasm. The working sessions were not in the same league with the socializing. A disappointed Wool would later report to fellow IAFA board members that the value of discussion had descended from the summit of their first session in Bahamas to a point of almost diminishing returns with their third meeting in Mexico.[34]

Though the conference achieved little from an intellectual point of view, it was highly successful in bringing together Latin American and U.S. writers, critics, and publishers. In Mexico Knopf met Rodríguez Monegal, who would later edit a two-volume *Borzoi Anthology of Latin American Literature* (1977) for him. It was also on that occasion that Parra met Laughlin and charmed him with his wit. In 1967 New Directions issued the Chilean's *Poems and Antipoems* in bilingual form. Altogether most of the Latin American guests must have shared Donoso's feelings: "This enthusiasm at seeing myself surrounded by so many legendary people whom I knew through their work may have been infantile and naïve but no less valid to me for that. . . . How could I not want Styron to speak to me of his literary drought . . .? Quickly these characters were transformed into people: they ate in front of me at the table."[35]

The symposia always broke up in a spirit of camaraderie. Behind the facade of anti-American rhetoric there was genuine Latin interest in gaining access to this country's cultural scene. Donoso described the Mexican symposium's closing with a fraternal party at the Fuentes home: "Kitty de Hoyos, a starlet of Mexican films, took the stiff, Puritan hand of Rodman Rockefeller and passed it over her hips, while behind his glasses, the Yankee millionaire's eyes bulged with surprise and acute sensation. . . . To the unforgettable sound of 'I Want to Hold Your Hand,' which could hardly be heard above the uproar, Erika Carlson, Arabela Arbenz . . . and China Mendoza were dancing wildly."[36]

The last conference, held in the elegant resort of Puerto Azul, had a larger guest list, which included even such rabidly anti-American figures as Cortázar and Uruguayan writer and critic Mario Benedetti. As for the American participants, Wool and his Venezuelan assistant José Guillermo Castillo invited Tad Szulc from the *New York Times*, Richard Rovere from the *New Yorker*, *Village Voice* editor Jack Newfield, and publisher Jason Epstein from the *New York Review of Books*, as well as authors Robert Lowell, Arthur Miller, Robert Penn Warren, and Elizabeth Hardwick.

IAFA did not proselytize. It simply encouraged delegates to participate in a free and relaxed discussion of inter-American matters, artistic and political. At Puerto Azul, for instance, Lowell and Parra read from each other's work and led a discussion about the "common poetic language" that ran through the Americas. At these conventions Latin American writers had a chance to meet some of the pushers and movers of the U.S. cultural scene and befriend some of them. No strings were attached; any topic was discussible. Even Cuban intellectuals were invited (none came) to the meetings. IAFA showed how intellectual freedom operated.[37]

Other than the symposia, IAFA's accomplishments were meager. The creation in 1965 of a bimonthly newsletter, *Mirador*, with Wool and Claudio Campuzano as editors, intended to keep Latin and U.S. readers abreast of the boom. Though modestly produced, the bilingual publication boasted a respectable roll of correspondents—Fuentes, Rodríguez Monegal, and Leopoldo Torres Nilson. When *Mundo Nuevo* began in 1966, *Mirador* closed down.

Wool and Castillo's chief concern was getting Latin American authors established in New York. They concentrated their efforts on organizing a play- and novel-translation program and introducing writers to New York publishers. Thanks to their initiative, Charles Scribner's Sons published Argentine Beatriz Guido's *End of a Day* in 1966 and Farrar, Straus and Giroux hired Argentine poet Alberto Girri as a consultant for Spanish language works. Though not directly involved with IAFA, Harper and Row also became interested in Latin American literature. At the behest of editor Roger Klein, in 1966 Harper and Row published Luis Harss and Barbara Dohmann's introduction to the boom, *Into the Mainstream.*

But not everyone approved of IAFA's record. Officials at the Pan American Union, an intergovernmental institution established in 1890, complained that IAFA was merely duplicating their efforts.[38] What the union bureaucrats failed to realize was that their timid diffusion of Latin American letters had only reached the few college professors who consulted their bibliographies. Their promotion of writers as agents of diplomatic exchange had done Latin American literature a poor service.

In 1967 IAFA merged with a new foundation, the Center for Inter-American relations. This institution would take up the promotion of Latin American authors where IAFA left off.

V

The chairman of the board of the newly founded center was David Rockefeller, who believed that IAFA's activities needed to be merged into a larger program. The center had a bigger staff and better funding. It was more ambitious in design and committed to creating a forum for Latin American literary, political, and economic issues on a more massive scope than its predecessor. The selection of the Payne Mansion at 680 Park Avenue as the center's headquarters epitomizes Rockefeller's approach. He wanted to move beyond IAFA's famed symposia and set up bolder cultural programs.

The Rockefeller brothers had endorsed Kennedy's Alliance for Progress with its intention of luring Latin Americans away from communism through massive development programs. Though they disagreed with the administration's emphasis on social change over the encouragement of private enterprise, they shared Kennedy's concern with Cuban penetration.[39] In this connection, the center's more sophisticated organization would constitute an effective instrument in offsetting leftist propaganda by molding a solid relationship with the rest of the western hemisphere's intellectual and business leaders.

In addition to Rockefeller, other members of the board included people who had held leading public positions in the area of Latin American policy. William D. Rogers, former U.S. deputy coordinator of the Alliance for Progress, became the center's first president. Its executive director was William MacLeish, son of poet Archibald MacLeish, who had served as assistant secretary of state for inter-American affairs under Roosevelt. Other participants were Lincoln Gordon, a former State Department official; René D' Harnoncourt, then director of the Museum of Modern Art; and Arthur O. Sulzberger, publisher of the *New York Times*.

One of the center's most successful undertakings was the creation of the Literature Program, which served as a conduit for quality Latin American writing in this country. Its director was former IAFA official José Guillermo Castillo. The Venezuelan was at home both in the New York publishing milieu and in Latin American literary circles. He often traveled south to study local literary scenes, and, unlike the more cautious Knopfs, he gave Americans the impression that the region was teeming with exciting fiction that anxiously awaited recognition.

Because of language barriers and the lack of a structured publishing network in South America, most American publishers were reluctant to explore Latin literary markets. The most pressing problem, however, was translation. Castillo set up a translation program in 1968 to simplify getting Latin American books into English. His staff worked to match up skilled translators with publishers, as well as to help in the training of new ones. Castillo's most important innovation was the establishment of a translation subsidy that helped publishers defray the cost of an English version of a Spanish or Portuguese language work. Often the center covered half of the translating expense. On rare occasions it would pay the whole cost, a sum ranging between $2,000 and $5,000. The center used a committee of critics and professors to select the books it would subsidize. The committee included Rodríguez Monegal; New York University professor of Spanish Alexander Coleman; Argentine critics Omar del Carlo and María Luisa Bastos, then living in New York; the *New Yorker* writer and translator Alastair Reid; prominent translator Gregory Rabassa; literary critic John Simon, and poet Mark Strand. The center submitted their reports and suggestions to publishers. In order to reassure hesitant editors, Castillo often accompanied the reports with sample European reviews of the books in question.

Castillo looked on translating a Latin American work and getting accepted by a New York publisher as just the first step in launching a work into the American mainstream. He schooled his protégés about New York publishing and the media. He wrote that at the beginning it was hard to break the ice because the situation in New York was simply chaotic and everybody had developed a 1930s mentality. He stated that publishers and editors did not even listen to him and hoped that God would spare and protect them from such an awful plague.[40] His persistence and knack for public relations, along with his charm and sense of humor, finally succeeded, however, in winning over dubious editors. An assistant recalled that Castillo placed many of the boom novels over lunch and at cocktail parties.

Along with the translation program, Castillo established a network of critics, reviewers, publishers, and professors who served as consultants for the center. In 1970 he hired Ronald Christ, a professor of English and comparative literature at Rutgers, to edit the center's literary journal, *Review*. The author of *The Narrow Act* (1969), a study on Borges's art of allusion, Christ turned out to be a fortunate choice. He was a resourceful and imaginative editor. His taste was flawless and his interest ranged from avant-garde literature and film to psychotherapy. The combination of Castillo's negotiating skills and Christ's extraordinary ability to spot good writing made the literature program a fruitful venture. Christ recalled that by the mid-seventies the center had made such an impact that the editors were calling on them and not vice versa.[41] The center also became an important source for researchers of Latin culture in this country. Even governmental agencies like the Unites States Information Agency relied on the expertise of those at the center. In 1976 they consulted the center on the logistics of organizing a successful conference of Latin American writers to be held in Mexico City.

Under Christ's editorship *Review* was an attractive publication. Earlier it had merely reprinted reviews of Latin American books that had appeared in American publications. The first issue came out in 1968 and was put together by Rodríguez Monegal. Alexander Coleman edited the 1969 number. Christ brought in a more attractive format and turned *Review* into a full-fledged literary publication. Starting in 1970 it appeared three times a year and included interviews with Latin American writers and artists, scholarly articles, and contributions by such authors as Cabrera Infante and fellow Cuban Octavio Armand. Most innovative was the "focus" section devoted to a specific work or author whose book had recently been published in the United States The first of these features focused on *One Hundred Years of Solitude*. Christ had reviewed the novel for *Commonweal* in 1970 and was bent on making the most of its bestseller status. *Review* capitalized on both the American and European triumph by reprinting a wide array of critical praises—from the *New York Times Book Review* to *La Quinzaine Litteraire* (Paris).

In 1971 Christ expanded the "focus" section to include a "chronology" or autobiographical piece designed to acquaint readers with an author's background. Finest among these sketches were those prepared by the writers themselves—Cabrera Infante's clever welcome to the English translation of his *Three Trapped Tigers* (1971); Puig's hailing of the appearance of *Betrayed by Rita Hayworth* (1971); and Donoso's memoir on *The Obscene Bird of the Night* (1973). Christ devoted entire issues to writers of classic status—Neruda (no. 11), Paz (no. 6), and Asturias (no. 15)—and still found plenty of room to boost younger and lesser-known figures, many of whom later went on to gain great recognition in the United States In fact, Christ's editorship and that of Gregory Kolovakos, who became his assistant in 1972, showed a strong attraction to the newer experimental writing done by, among others, Cabrera Infante, Severo Sarduy, Lezama Lima, and Brazilian Nelida Piñón. *Review*'s attention meant a great deal to these writers, as is revealed by Cabrera Infante's comments to Christ after the "focus" devoted to *Three Trapped Tigers*. He said that it was also very good of him to have displayed his features (or *vera effigies*) so prominently on the starting line and that he hoped he did not get crucified for this by the other 10,000 Latin American writers who thought they should be there.[42]

Review analyzed Latin American writing and culture as no other English-language journal did. The magazine was the first to publish in the United States articles on Macedonio Fernández, a twenties Argentine experimental author, Puig, and Sarduy. Christ opened the journal to younger critics and to scholars not connected to the field, like film critic Andrew Sarris from the *Village Voice*, whose "Rerunning Puig and Cabrera Infante" appeared in the fall 1973 issue.

Christ's *Review* shaped an exciting inter-American dialogue. By making available in English articles written for Latin audiences (for example, Vargas Llosa's and Cortázar's interpretations of Lezama Lima's *Paradiso*, Borges's introduction to Herman Melville's "Bartleby the Scrivener") and by encouraging U.S. critics to write about Hispanic authors (Dore Ashton's "Octavio Paz and Words and Images" and Paul West's reading of Carpentier's fiction), *Review* reached out to a wider American audience, showing that readers did not need to know Spanish to appreciate Latin American culture. Indeed, *Review* did what *Mundo Nuevo* had hoped to accomplish years earlier. It communicated with the larger American intellectual community and advanced the idea that Latin America was producing genuinely innovative literature.

The combined issue 21 and 22 of *Review* in 1979 was the last edited by Christ. He decided to leave the center because of a mixture of political and artistic intrigue. In 1977 he had accepted a Fulbright lectureship in Chile. A group led by disaffected *Review* contributors launched a campaign to prevent his trip and argued that such travel implied an endorsement of the Chilean military regime. While Christ was in Santiago, the contributors resigned from the editorial board of *Review* and forced him to hasten his return to New York. Though the center supported him, the incident destroyed the consensus among collaborators and supporters of the magazine and eventually led to Christ's resignation. Several months later Roger Stone invited him to reassume the directorship, but Christ declined. His departure took from the center a diligent promoter of the newest and most avant-garde Latin American authors. Christ had ably taken on Castillo's role when the Venezuelan moved back to Caracas in around 1976 to open an art gallery. He was counted on to help promote new books and make a splash, as is indicated in a 1977 letter from José Donoso, who had three titles coming out in New York at about the same time. Donoso told Christ that he was terribly excited and that he had a good feeling that this time he was going to modestly hit the jackpot with all these books coming out so beautifully scaled. He said he knew that Christ would husband lovingly the reviewers and writers and would determine who should get it and what they should say about it.[43]

Christ's editorship was turned over to Luis Harss, a senior lecturer of Spanish at the University of West Virginia. Harss found space for the more peripheral figures of Latin American letters and encouraged more specialized contributions. He published articles on Argentine Mario Satz, contemporary Chilean writing, and other barely known authors. As a result of this approach, *Review* lost its currency and vitality and became more of a conventional academic journal. Yet the plight of the magazine was largely due to the problems affecting the literature program in the wake of the Christ case. After 1979 the center was continually undergoing reorganizations that bewildered its staff. Such upheavals made editing *Review* a difficult task. Harss was ordered to reduce the number of pages drastically and had to wage a constant battle over budget cuts to keep the magazine alive. At the same time he was put in the uncomfortable position of having to constantly warn contributors that materials might be subject to delays or cutting. In 1982 *Review* temporarily ceased publication. Its end came suddenly when Cuban-exiled writers led by Reinaldo Arenas accused Harss of pro-leftist bias and forced his resignation. Their bone of contention was that *Review* no. 30 focused on literature and exile and had disregarded the Cubans' plight, and concentrated on pro-Marxist figures like critic Angel Rama and Julio Cortázar—who had not been forced to leave their native countries, but had chosen to live abroad. *Review* resumed publication in 1984 under an editorial board, which was replaced in 1985 by the current editor Alfred MacAdam (starting with no. 34).

Other important center collaborators were Rodríguez Monegal, Alexander Coleman, Alastair Reid, Gregory Rabassa, translators Thomas Colchie and Suzanne Jill Levine, novelist William Kennedy, and Columbia University professor Frank MacShane. Though in the late sixties he was a relative newcomer to the American scene, Rodríguez Monegal made an invaluable contribution because of his close ties with boom and post-boom circles; Alfred Knopf rightly called him the high priest of Latin American letters.[44] Rodríguez Monegal contributed spirited essays on Neruda's *Residence on Earth*, Cortázar, Lezama Lima, Puig, Severo Sarduy, and Mexican novelist Gustavo Sainz. Unfortunately, his connection with the center ended rather precipitously in 1976 when he resigned from the advisory board of the Literature Program over differences with editor Ronald Christ.

Alexander Coleman had taken up the cause of contemporary Latin novelists at a time when few colleagues dared to venture beyond 1950. In 1966 he began reviewing for the *New York Times Book Review*; through Rodríguez Monegal he became a member of the Literature Program's board of advisors. At Castillo's request he created and taught a course on modern Latin American fiction for New York University's "Sunrise Semester," broadcast by CBS in 1972. The program, aired across the United States, was co-sponsored by the center.

In spite of his involvement in a myriad of projects besides those of the center, Alastair Reid willingly cooperated with Castillo. A Scotsman, Reid had fallen in love with Latin American literature in the fifties when he was living in Spain and dating an Argentine woman who introduced him to Borges's work. He was troubled by the indifference toward Latin American authors in the English-speaking world: "When I first translated . . . Borges, some 14 years ago [in the midfifties], four publishers expressed positive disinterest—not just in Borges, but in Latin American writers in general."[45] In 1964 he traveled in South America and befriended, among others, Pablo Neruda whose work he translated in 1969. By the late sixties, Hispanic novelists and poets occupied a great deal of his attention: "London and Paris have quite a concentration of Latin Americans. . . . In London, I probably see more Latin American than I do English people, from choice."[46] In Paris, he assisted Rodríguez Monegal and later Castillo in assembling a list of Latin American works most in need of translation.

At the center Reid helped set the standards for good translation, which became the hallmark of the books subsidized by the Literature Program. He also deserves credit for slipping many articles about Latin American literature and art into the *New Yorker*, for which he has written since 1951. He arranged a "first reading" contract between Borges and the magazine in 1969. Borges's former translator Norman Thomas Di Giovanni observed that Alastair Reid had gotten him and Borges in the *New Yorker* through a crack in the door that had taken him five years to open.[47] Though less active at the center, Rabassa helped make its Literature Program a success through his superb translations. Over a period of twenty years, he made accessible to American readers such classics as *Hopscotch* (1966) and *One Hundred Years of Solitude* (1970). When Rabassa joined the advisory board, he brought with him impeccable credentials, including a 1967 National Book Award for Translation for *Hopscotch*. He considered the Literature Program to be a valuable asset to Hispanic writing. His association with the center worked in two ways. He came to Castillo's rescue when he desperately needed a translator for Lezama Lima's baroque *Paradiso* (1974) and willingly contributed to make Asturias's *The Green Pope* (1971) a more readable book in English. In return, the center listened to his pleas and promoted the publication of such obscure novels as *Macho Camacho's Beat* (1981) by Puerto Rican Luis Rafael Sanchez and *Seven Serpents and Seven Moons* by Ecuadorian Demetrio Aguilera Malta. In the latter case, Rabassa had special reasons for wanting the book published. His wife, Clementine, had written her dissertation on the Ecuadorian and believed that he deserved a boost. Thanks to Rabassa, the center negotiated with the University of Texas Press to have the novel published and financed the translation. Like Reid, Rabassa deplored the meager recognition accorded to translators by both publishers and critics. In his case, however, the problem was overcome. By the mid-seventies, he had become a celebrity and had his hands full of more books than he could translate.

Among minor center figures, Suzanne Jill Levine and Thomas Colchie deserve mention. Levine, a former student of Coleman at New York University and a close friend of Rodríguez Monegal, began her career at the center and collaborated with it until the late seventies. She wrote regularly for *Review* and was commissioned to translate Manuel Puig's *Betrayed by Rita Hayworth* (1973) and *Heartbreak Tango* (1973), which were the most important of her assignments.

Like Rodríguez Monegal and Rabassa, Colchie was determined to give a fair share of attention to Brazilian writers. For him the center was a springboard to bigger and better things. In 1976 Colchie became literary agent for young, untranslated Brazilians—Marcio Souza, Ivan Angelo, and others—and persuaded Bard/Avon's executive director, Robert Wyatt, to strengthen his Latin American paperback reprints list with a series of original translations. Pleased with the outcome, Wyatt contracted in 1981 for new English translations of Guimarães Rosa's *Sertão: Veredas* and some of Jorge Amado's novels, which had previously been in the hands of Knopf.

The publishers most receptive to Castillo and Christ's boom writers were Wyatt, Roger Straus of Farrar, Straus and Giroux; Cass Canfield, Jr. of Harper and Row; John Macrae of E. P. Dutton; and Boston publisher David Godine. Of the whole group, Straus was certainly the most active. In hiring Andre Conrad and later David Rieff, he pioneered a trend that resulted in the proliferation of full-time Spanish and Portuguese editors in New York publishing houses. As a member of the center's board of directors, he followed closely the fortunes of *Review* and the translation program. Straus believed in the commercial value of friendships between U.S. and Latin American authors. Carlos Fuentes, one of his writers, had used his contacts with William Styron, Arthur Miller, and Jack Gelber to become a celebrity in this country. Straus encouraged center officials to make sure luminaries like Susan Sontag or John Updike appeared in their panels and parties.

At Harper and Row, Canfield welcomed Latin Americans because of his wife, Italian-born Gabriela Brufani. Before moving to New York, Brufani had lived in Peru and traveled often to Buenos Aires. There she had met Victoria Ocampo's godchild, Pipina Prieto, who for years kept her informed about Latin American writing. Eventually, this led to Harper and Row's impressive Latin list, which included García Márquez, Vargas Llosa, Cabrera Infante, and Reinaldo Arenas. This was quite a reversal of opinion for a publishing house that in 1955 had turned down Juan Rulfo's *Pedro Páramo* (1953), a wonderful example of magical realism, because "it is essentially a rambling book which does not seem to add up to enough in the end—at least enough for American readers."[48]

It was mostly thanks to Castillo's labor of persuasion that Macrae and E. P. Dutton came to the field of Latin American publishing. Dutton began with Borges's *The Book of Imaginary Beings* (1969), which fared quite well. The most ambitious undertaking was probably Wyatt's at Avon/Bard; its line of Latin American paperbacks has grown steadily since it began in the late seventies.

In addition to these commercial presses, the center allied itself with university presses. At the University of Texas Press, poet Lysander Kemp actively supported the publication of Hispanic books. The Latin American series first debuted in 1960 when Houston based Pan American Sulphur Company set up a fund designed to defray the production costs of Latin American books. The program received additional backing when University of Texas Press became the principal beneficiary of a Rockefeller Foundation grant intended to cover translation expenses. Over a ten-year period the Pan American Series printed works by Borges, Rulfo, and Paz, among other eminent authors. Later, when the grant was depleted, the press welcomed center-supported books like José María Arguedas's *Deep Rivers* (1978). Other university presses that collaborated were those of Columbia University, New York University, University of Oklahoma. Columbia University Press, at Christ's suggestion, published a wide selection of titles, including Donoso's *The Boom in Spanish American Literature* (1977) and collections of poems by lesser-known figures like Nicaraguans Pablo Antonio Cuadra and José Emilio Pacheco. Because of disappointing sales—as of April 1981 Pacheco and Donoso's paperbacks had sold 1,036 and 896 copies, respectively—Columbia discontinued the series.[49]

Some renowned New York critics and reviewers also responded to the center's call. Novelist William Kennedy often persuaded editors at *Quest* and the *New Republic* to assign him reviews of new Latin American books. At the *New York Times*, Nona Balakian readily satisfied Christ's request that she find sympathetic reviewers. What really saved the day for the Latin Americans, though, were editors John Leonard and Edwin McDowell. Their usually admiring remarks served to offset the cooler comments of their colleague Anatole Broyard, who dismissed Donoso's *Sacred Families and Charleston* (1977) in these contemptuous terms: "He describes his native tongue as rich—yet in his novellas, the language is meager, fussy, deracinated and marred by clichés. Perhaps in moving from Chile to Barcelona he lost his tongue."[50]

At the *New York Review of Books* editor Bob Silvers had taken up the cause of Latin writers in the mid-seventies. The center exercised clout at the journal through Columbia University professor of English Michael Wood, who was both a regular contributor and a member of *Review*'s advisory board. Other regular reviewers of center products were John Simon at Book World and poet Mark Strand. Christ himself reviewed frequently for *Commonweal*.

VI

At first view, Borges is perhaps the least South American of the writers who established themselves in the United States in the late sixties. Though he was one of the chief mentors of the boom writers, his politics, his genius, and his American career were all strikingly different. At home, the Argentine's distaste for regionalism and leftist or nationalist causes had provoked resentment in the literary circles of the thirties and forties. Only the *Sur* coterie revered his talent. His addiction to English books and world civilization—"I believe our tradition is all of Western culture"[51]—hindered his recognition outside Argentina, for these traits contravened traditional perceptions of Latin American writing as naturalistic and local.

The early stages of Borges's American career were curiously expressive of his own modest and self-effacing nature. As we saw in chapters 1 and 2, he was dismissed both by Waldo Frank and Blanche Knopf. The first Americans to recognize his genius were, incredibly, the editors of *Ellery Queen's Mystery Magazine*, who in 1940 ran "The Garden of Forking Paths," a story that on one level can be read as detective fiction. In 1948 poet Ruth Stephan's short-lived magazine, *The Tiger's Eye*, published "The Lottery of Babylon." A year later, at the behest of translator Mary Wells, James Laughlin included "An Examination of the Work of Herbert Quain" and "The Circular Ruins" in the 1949 *New Directions* (no. 11) anthology.[52] At the same time *Partisan Review* printed "Emma Zunz" and "The Zahir." Almost ten years later little magazines like *Prairie Schooner* began to "discover" Borges.

Belated American recognition contrasts sharply with Borges's French career. As early as 1930 Valéry Larbaud and other Parisian critics acknowledged the value of his work. In 1952 Roger Caillois published his *Ficciones* in "La Croix du Sud" series in a translation by Argentine Nestor Ibarra.[53] Traditionally, U.S. publishers look to their French counterparts for their foreign-language books. In the case of Borges, the Paris–New York network did not work. Then in 1961, Borges shared with Samuel Beckett the International Publishers Prize (Prix Formen-

tor). The following year two publishers issued overlapping anthologies
of his fictions: Evergreen–Grove printed *Ficciones* in Alastair Reid's
and Anthony Kerrigan's translation; New Directions published
Labyrinths, one of the best collections of his work. It was put together
by Michigan State University professor of Spanish Donald Yates and
Princeton University professor of Spanish and Latin American literature
James Irby. Both books garnered dazzling reviews that equated Borges's
genius with that of Joyce, Kafka, and Nabokov.

In 1964 University of Texas Press issued *Dreamtigers* and *Other In-
quisitions*. Borges had been an Edward L. Tinker professor at the University of Texas Spanish Department in 1961. Two years later professor
Miguel Enguídanos persuaded his colleague Mildred Boyer, who had
published a collection of Borges's translations in *Texas Quarterly*, to
translate *El hacedor* (1960) (*Dreamtigers*). Boyer worked with the prose
pieces, and British poet Harold Morland translated the poems. *Other In-
quisitions* was turned into English by translator Ruth Simms. Unlike
Boyer's scrupulous attention to syntax, Simms's version seemed less
precise. University of Texas Press consultant James Irby observed that
her translations were often not careful enough and smoothed out some
of Borges's most striking devices, which can be rendered with reasonable accuracy in English.[54]

Of the two collections, *Dreamtigers* was the more successful. It sold
"fully as well" as the publishers had expected.[55] Critically, it surpassed
all predictions. Not only were reviews not assigned to Latin American
specialists, but critics hardly mentioned Borges's national origin. Paul
de Man in the *New York Times Book Review* appropriately la-
bled his piece "A Modern Master." He seemed particularly impressed
by Borges's laying bare the devices of his narrative: "For all their variety of tone and setting, the different stories all have a similar point of
departure. . . . They are about the style in which they are written."[56]
De Man understood Borges within a structuralist and post-structuralist
context. He argued that language is the sole standard by which to judge
Borges and looked ahead to the more "deconstructive" readings of his
fictions that became popular in the late seventies. The essay "Borges
and I" elicited this response: "The creation of beauty thus begins as an
act of duplicity. The writer engenders another self that is his mirror-like
reversal. In this anti self, the virtues and the vices of the original are curiously distorted and reversed."[57]

Less academic, but equally appreciative was *Time*'s recognition. At
the end of 1964 it listed *Dreamtigers* among the most notable books of

this century. But perhaps the supreme example of the unprecedented success of Borges's first five American books was the impact he had among well-known writers. In the *New Yorker*, John Updike pondered the Argentine's timely arrival and the solutions he could offer to a genre in crisis: "The question is . . . whether or not Borges's lifework . . . can serve . . . as any kind of clue to the way out of the dead-end narcissism and downright trashiness of present American fiction."[58] Interestingly, Updike fit Borges's work into the American literary tradition. The "fervent narrowness" of his style, Updike implied, has affinities with the Anglo-American commitment to lean prose. He found resonances of Hawthorne and Melville in Borges's use of the "oniric and hallucinatory," and of Wallace Stevens in the "meditative circularity" of Borges's poems.[59] In 1967 John Ashbery reviewed *Personal Anthology*, issued by Grove. An abstract and private poet himself, Ashbery found in the Argentine a kindred spirit, a writer for writers: "Of course, there is no reason to believe that his book is intended for the 'general reader' . . . in view of the examples of literary duplicity that abound in his work."[60]

Updike had hinted that Borges's works might be helpful to "blocked" American writers. The first to acknowledge such help was John Barth. Racked as he was at the time with the issue of "used-upness" of literary forms, he applauded Borges's creative use of "felt ultimacies" in "Pierre Menard, Author of the Quixote" in his 1967 essay "The Literature of Exhaustion": "[Borges] writes a remarkable and original work of literature, the implicit theme of which is the difficulty, perhaps the unnecessity, of writing original works of literature. His artistic victory . . . is that he confronts an intellectual dead-end and employs it against itself to accomplish a new human work."[61]

By the late sixties critics were arguing that American fiction had entered a "Borgesian" phase. According to Morris Dickstein, the transposition of history and personal identity into fantasy in the work of Barth, Donald Barthelme, Thomas Pynchon, and John Hawkes was clearly a product of Borges's influence.[62] Ronald Christ's *Paris Review* interview with Borges in 1967 confirmed the author's importance.[63]

When the center provided $1,500 toward the translation of Borges's *Book of Imaginary Beings*, which was contracted by Dutton in 1968, it was no longer trying to make a case for his value; it was trying to establish an official Borges canon in English. The instigator of the project was poet Norman Thomas Di Giovanni, who for eight years served as Borges's translator and literary agent. Di Giovanni had met Borges at

Harvard when the latter held the Charles Eliot Norton chair of poetry in the fall of 1967. Di Giovanni, dissatisfied with earlier translations, moved to Buenos Aires and worked for almost three years in collaboration with Borges. He commented to Castillo that he and Borges were in complete agreement on fundamental translation principles and felt they would come out with an English story and style that would be exactly like Borges intended. For both it was a rare, if not unique, opportunity to have author and translator working this way, and Di Giovanni believed that everything should be done to promote what they were doing.[64]

When *The Book of Imaginary Beings* appeared in 1969, Castillo and editors at Dutton embarked on a publicity campaign. A reticent Borges was made to read poems before a large audience at the YMCA in New York. The reception following at the center boasted such luminaries as Updike, Richard Howard, and Howard Moss, poetry editor at the *New Yorker*.

As with *Dreamtigers*, reviewers succumbed to Borges's craft. Perhaps the most lucid response came from novelist and philosopher William Gass in the *New York Review of Books*: "If, as Wittgenstein thought, 'philosophy is a battle against the bewitchment of our intelligence by means of language,' then Borges's prose, at least, performs a precisely similar function, for there is scarcely a story which is not built upon a sophistry . . . so fanatically embraced . . . it becomes the principal truth in the world his parables create . . . and we are compelled to wonder again whether we are awake or asleep . . . a dreamer or ourselves a dream."[65]

At Dutton, Borges's editor Marian Skedgell rejoiced; she knew such critical effusions paid off in concrete sales. By mid-1970 the book was into a second printing and arrangements were made for the publishing of a paperback edition.

John Macrae's intention of publishing Borges's earlier book *Historia universal de la infamia* (1935) threatened to upset Di Giovanni's fastidious timing of Borges's career in this country. In Di Giovanni's eyes, the book was not strong enough to maintain the momentum of success Borges had reached. Once more Castillo intervened; he managed to twist Macrae's arm, and *The Aleph and Other Stories* (1970) was issued instead. Geoffry Hartman's article in the *New York Times Book Review* turned the collection into yet another success. Like Gass, Hartman was agog at Borges's undermining of our notions of reality: "His humorous realism—names, dates, and nature-motifs formulaicallly introduced—is a pseudo-realism. Even the gaucho stories, for all their local color, are fantasies."[66]

Euphoria over Borges's work continued throughout the seventies. *Dr. Brodie's Report* (1972) and the parodic *Chronicles of Bustos Domecq* (1976) greatly impressed critics. A literary biography by Rodríguez Monegal appeared in 1978. Borges was so idolized that even a champion of socially committed literature like Alfred Razin felt compelled to come to terms with him. Confessedly bewildered, Kazin portrayed his interview with the Argentine as a meeting of a "mind—visibly in the process of composition. . . . [Borges] is as strange in the flesh as he is on the page."[67] No less taken aback was V. S. Naipaul, who feared that the critical enthusiasm was so "bogus that it obscures his greatness."[68] Whatever Naipaul's apprehensions, no Latin American writer has left a deeper imprint in this country than Borges. For one thing, Borges redefined the course of inter-American literary relations. Up to 1960 the tide of influence was mostly one sided—Whitman on Neruda and Ruben Darío, Poe on Quiroga, Faulkner on Rulfo. Borges became the first major Latin American literary influence on U.S. writers. Critic Tony Tanner found the effect of Borges's fantastic conjurings on writers as diverse as Barth, Robert Coover, and Mary McCarthy: "A part of the appeal that Borges has for American writers is his sense that 'reality' is an infinitely plural affair, that there are many different worlds and that the intersection points might not be so fixed as some people think, that the established ways in which we classify and order reality are as much 'fictions' as his stories."[69]

Borges's impact recast the image of the Latin American writer. Before Borges most Americans and Europeans read Latin American literature principally to learn about the region. Borges's craft shattered those expectations. By placing his art in the wider framework of Western culture, he made the question of nationality of little interest. Though not all Latin American novelists who followed him into fame disguise their actual background to the extent Borges does, the response to his "fictions" has affected the reception of their work. After Borges, one reads García Márquez or Fuentes less for what they tell us about Latin American culture than for what they offer as writers of fiction.

Di Giovanni believed that Borges's fame could spread to other Argentine writers. In 1969 he sent editor Harry Ford of Atheneum a prospectus of a collection he and Borges wished to edit. The anthology included writers like Cortázar and Ernesto Sábato, among a list of twenty. The translator had miscalculated; in the late sixties there was not a broad enough interest to launch such a project. Both Atheneum and Houghton Mifflin turned it down. Di Giovanni's efforts on behalf of Borges's friend and collaborator, Adolfo Bioy Casares, were no more successful. Bioy is a major writer in the fantastic-satirical vein, and his obscurity outside Buenos Aires irked Di Giovanni because he felt that he should stand on his own feet and separate from Borges for his association with Borges was hurting him. Borges even told Di Giovanni that he knew people who thought Bioy was a Borges invention.[70] What triggered Di Giovanni's interest in an American career for Bioy was the praise his *Asleep in the Sun* (1968) had garnered while Di Giovanni was in Buenos Aires. But in New York, Di Giovanni's championing of Bioy left Roger Straus and Harry Ford cold. Bioy Casares, they argued, lacked French endorsement and did not fit the image of a Latin American author. Di Giovanni abandoned Bioy, leaving his fortunes to the tenacious Castillo. Almost eight years went by before the Venezuelan prevailed upon Dutton and had another of Bioy's books, *A Plan for Escape* (1975), published. In 1978 the center supported *Asleep in the Sun* (1978), translated by Suzanne Jill Levine. Both books had difficulty winning recognition. As Di Giovanni feared, Bioy seemed fated to be known solely as Borges's witty coauthor of *Six Problems for Don Isidro Parodi* (1980) and the *Chronicles of Bustos Domecq*.

In the mid-seventies, the Borges–Di Giovanni connection was broken. There are no clear accounts of the abrupt breakup. It is evident that the parting of ways happened amid much upset and misunderstanding.

While Borges's books enjoyed a huge success, he himself, as a personality on the American scene, was self-obliterating. Nothing could be more different than Carlos Fuentes's style. Unlike the Argentine, Fuentes was deliberate and unrelenting in his efforts to smash his way into New York's intellectual circles. Fuentes's high-living cosmopolitanism differs strikingly from Borges's refined aestheticism. Fuentes's stance has a public and political dimension to it. He enjoys flaunting his familiarity with Joyce, Nabokov, or Styron as much as he does censuring American foreign policy or playing the spokesman for all of Latin America. His American career is a good example of a Latin author bedeviled by multiple and often conflicting allegiances—to his own culture, the Western avant-garde, leftist causes, and the joys of capitalistic publishing. As critic Keith Botsford remarked, "He is too sophisticated to play the kind of role that the Left would like to force on him, but he is also too rational, and perhaps too ambitious, not to take advantage of it; he is certainly too self-aware to let others create his parts, but he is also impulsive and desirous enough to want to be both in and out."[71]

Earlier than fellow boom members, Fuentes realized that American recognition was the most crucial, and profitable, step in the process of dissemination of Latin American letters. The son of a diplomat, Fuentes grew up in Washington, D.C., and Santiago, Chile. His formidable command of English and international upbringing had much to do with his rapid success in America.

In the late fifties, Fuentes received a grant from the Centro Mejicano de Escritores to work on the novel *Where the Air is Clear* (1958). The director of the Rockefeller-funded organization, Margaret Shedd, and her assistant Donald Demarest did their best to promote the novel in the United States. When editor Simon Bessie at Harper and Row rejected it, Demarest warned him: "[The novel] has earmarks of a potential seller. And if it is I'll try to refrain from gloating."[72] As it turned out, Bessie's decision was wrong; Fuentes's novel was well received when it appeared in 1968 in the United States, and his career ascended fast.

What really opened doors to Fuentes was his friendship with *Newsweek* editor John Gerossi. A member of the New Left, Gerossi sympathized with Fuentes's pro-Castro leanings of the time and introduced him to New York literary agent Carl Brandt. The connection made a difference. Brandt realized that his client was blessed with enough gifts—sophisticated handling of modernistic narrative techniques and solid liberal credentials—to charm the hip elements of the American literary establishment. The agent's dream came true in an unexpected way when the State Department refused to issue Fuentes a visa to enter the country to participate in an NBC debate with Richard Goodwin, Kennedy's Latin American advisor, and the Mexican became a media star—a martyr of the anti-establishment. Lee Baxandall in *Studies on the Left* used the occasion to run a long interview. with Fuentes giving his political views. The piece focused on Fuentes's admiration of C. Wright Mills and on his contempt for U.S. "intellectual provincialism."[73] Fuentes's next novel, *The Death of Artemio Cruz*, appeared in 1964. Although it was one of his best books, Fuentes's new publisher, Roger Straus, also reaped the benefits of the author's controversial image. Reviewers, for the most part, overlooked the author's skillful interlocking of narrative voices and dwelt on the novel's depiction of the political corruption of a revolutionary "caudillo."

The reviewer for the *New Yorker* was an exception. His incisive reading captured Fuentes's powerful characterization as well as his problems with *Artemio Cruz*: "The confusion of voices, along with the fiddled up time sequence, creates an effect not of modernity but of the sort of confusion that was visible in the work of the generation of academic painters who were jolted by Cubism into an attempt to keep abreast of the new wave."[74] This view was shared by critic John Brown, then cultural attaché in Mexico, who refused to review the novel for the *New York Times* on the grounds that it was mediocre. The novel did well commercially. Blanche Knopf's comment sheds light on Fuentes's rising popularity at the time: "We perhaps made a mistake never getting after Fuentes' *Artemio Cruz* which is getting a very good press here despite you (Brown) not liking it."[75]

With *Aura* (1965), a gothic novella deftly translated by Lysander Kemp, Fuentes experienced a setback. Even an admirer like Alexander Coleman deemed it a "thin book in every sense."[76] Critical displeasure, however, did not hinder Fuentes's good fortune in the United States. By the mid-sixties only Jorge Amado could boast of having more titles translated into English. Certainly Fuentes's ability to hobnob on equal terms with famous authors helped his case: "He was the first to have friendship with important writers. . . . James Jones loans him his apartment on the Ile St. Louis, Mandriargues and William Styron receive him as a friend."[77]

The controversial image he enjoyed at home where he had denounced the Mexican government's repression of students in 1968 and "caciquismo" in Michapa carried over to the New York appearance of *A Change of Skin* (1968), translated by Sam Hileman. The novel had been a hit in Italy and enjoyed a *succès de scandale* in Spain where censors banned it for its "pornographic, communistic" qualities.[78] With the exception of critic David Gallagher in the *New York Times Book Review*, who questioned Fuentes's "hipster-existentialist, sub-Mailerish philosophy," most New York reviewers praised his "virtuosity" and urbanity.[79] A second run-in with American immigration authorities in 1969 boosted the popularity of the novel. When barred from landing in Puerto Rico, he appealed to his New York agent. He wrote that from the decks he could see a land that was his, part of Latin America, but an occupied land he could not set foot on. He wondered if perhaps some appropriate noises should be made.[80] Straus and Brandt swiftly mobilized writers in his support. At the 1969 National Book Award press conference Alfred Kazin read a resolution deploring the Immigration Service's action. American P.E.N. and the Authors League in telegrams to the Secretary of State called the incident simply "shocking." The case also drew support from Senator William Fulbright, who urged the Nixon administration to allow the entrance of aliens otherwise excluded because of their leftist affiliations. These plans were bolstered by petitions drawn up by the center and Straus.

The early seventies found Fuentes working in a grandiose, baroque vein. The outcome was his encyclopedic novel *Terra Nostra* (1976). Translated by Margaret Sayers Peden, it appeared in English shortly after it received Mexico's coveted Javier Villaurrutia Prize in 1975. The novel probes Mexico's Iberian past in an attempt to understand its present circumstances. It is a good example of what critic Wendy Faris calls the author's penchant for cross-fertilizing literature with intellectual history.[81] Though Fuentes rightly considered it his most important novel and was said to have threatened to stop writing and put up an enchilada booth if it displeased critics, Brandt feared the book's arcane prose might impair American reception. The center turned down the request for a translation subsidy but provided publicity backup. *Review* ran a focus on *Terra Nostra* in issue 19, which aroused advance curiosity. Christ offered to arrange a publication party fitting the book: "Perhaps we could plan something a little grander than usual, maybe in cooperation with George Plimpton and Roger Straus."[82] The *New York Times* ran an interview that stressed Fuentes's dual role as artist and Mexican ambassador to France.[83] When the novel appeared most reviewers agreed that it was his most audacious performance. Robert Coover in the *New York Times Book Review* and Michael Wood in the *New York Review of Books* were equally impressed by the novel's rich prose and massive scope.[84]

After *Terra Nostra*, Fuentes started working very closely with Sayers Peden to make his novels available in English almost simultaneously with their Spanish publication. His later novels *Distant Relations* (1982), *Old Gringo* (1985), *Christopher Unborn* (1989), and *The Orange Tree* (1993) appeared in this manner.

Today Fuentes is a much sought after novelist, sociocultural critic, television guest, and commencement speaker. He is considered to be an authority on Latin America and has been a consultant and think tank fellow. The Mexican has readily accepted his status as an international celebrity.

Undoubtedly the most prominent beneficiary of Fuentes's efforts to help the careers of fellow boomers was Gabriel García Márquez. The Colombian arrived in Mexico in 1961 when the boom coterie was beginning to coalesce. Fuentes's "team," as he called it, rescued him from poverty and anonymity.[85] While he was working on *One Hundred Years of Solitude*, Fuentes alerted critics that García Márquez had a masterpiece in store. By 1967, when the book was published in Buenos Aires, García Márquez's name was on everyone's lips in Spain and Latin America. His former friend Vargas Llosa recalled that the new editions "appeared at the astounding rate of one a week."[86]

In the United States, García Márquez's first book, the novella *No One Writes to the Colonel* (1968) had little success. Like that book, *One Hundred Years of Solitude* had a modest start. Going against Harper and Row's outside readers, who recommended against publication, Gabriela Canfield had written an evaluation that convinced her husband to publish the book. Her candid enthusiasm—"For me this is one of the best books I have read in a long time"[87]—was soon corroborated when the novel was awarded the best foreign book prize by the Academie Française in 1969.

The center paid for Gregory Rabassa's translation. García Márquez was adamant in his belief that only Rabassa was fit for the job and waited while the translator finished Manuel Mujica Laínez's *Bomarzo*. In four months Rabassa produced what is perhaps the most outstanding English rendering of a Latin American novel. The translator attributed his success to the novelist's classical, almost Cervantesque Spanish: "He doesn't fool around with syntax. . . . He uses the right word in the right place."[88]

Canfield worried about finding a sympathetic reviewer in the *New York Times* and asked Castillo to suggest Coleman.[89] As it turned out, his concern proved to be superfluous. The novel received euphoric acclaim. The first paperback edition made the best seller list of the *Times* for many weeks in 1971 and has continued to sell well ever since. In writing about it most reviewers hailed it as a tour de force. Ronald Christ in *Commonweal* argued that the book was the ultimate proof that the novel was "fantastically alive."[90] John Leonard in the *New York Times Book Review* compared García Márquez to Nabokov and Gunther Grass.[91] In the *New York Review of Books* Jack Richardson spoke of its cathartic effects: "When the book ends with its sudden self-knowledge and its intimations of holocaust, we are left with that pleasant exhaustion which only very great novels seem to provide."[92] Paul West's comments in *Book World* bordered on the ecstatic and likened the author's storytelling to a "verbal Mardi Gras."[93] *One Hundred Years of Solitude* skipped the usual stages of recognition. As Alastair Reid remarked, "the book was immediately moved by reviewers beyond criticism into that essential literary experience occupied by *Alice in Wonderland* and *Don Quixote.* Invoked as a classic, in a year it became a classic."[94] The novel's appeal was broad. On the one hand, readers who had never before encountered a Latin American novel were enchanted by García Márquez's fiery lovers and rain of yellow flowers. On the other, writers like John Hawkes and Barth thought Macondo—García Márquez's counterpart to Faulkner's Yoknapatawpha county—surpassed the original: "I read Faulkner with proper astonishment. . . . I do not remember him with great pleasure," Barth said. "Yet . . . the things that bother me in Faulkner I admire when I see them in Márquez."[95] Barth's remark accounted perhaps for an important element in his American triumph. García Márquez had deftly fused the narrative modes of his acknowledged mentors—Hemingway's compressed prose and Faulkner's grandiloquent vision.

The fame of *One Hundred Years of Solitude* directed attention to his earlier work. In 1972 Harper and Row published *Leaf Storm and Other Stories* (1955), also in Rabassa's translation. Though the collection was greeted with less fanfare, the publication of a new novel, *The Autumn of the Patriarch* (1976), a portion of which first appeared in the *New Yorker*, brought him back to the front rank. The Joycean novel about a solitary Caribbean dictator was also turned into English by Rabassa, who in 1977 won the P.E.N. Translation award for his performance. Part of the book's acclaim can be attributed to Harper and Row's timing: "Cass Canfield," commented Rabassa, "has been on my tail, because he wants it out in October. That would be an admirable date because, as I understand it, Gabo [García Márquez] will be at Columbia with Frank MacShane during the fall semester [1976] and available for all kinds of interviews and iconizings."[96]

The Autumn of the Patriarch, by far García Márquez's most explicitly political work, foregrounded his unabashedly Castroist sympathies. Castro's name was conspicuously absent from the list of Latin American dictators—Perón, Batista, Somoza—the novelist cited as sources for his book. In the aftermath of this publication, American media gave a great deal of space to García Márquez's extraliterary personality. Along with his perceptions of Latin American politics—"Progress in Latin America lies with Fidel Castro"—his love-hate affair with the United States seemed to be a favored topic. The author enjoyed fretting over his difficulties in entering the country as much as he did in praising the vitality of contemporary American culture: "There is no way one can relate to contemporary cultural life without going to the United States

. . . [It is the place] with the most serious students and the best analyses of my work."[97] The Nobel Prize García Márquez received in 1982 made him the symbol of Latin America's literary flowering. It enhanced the role of writer-politician that he shares with Fuentes. But just as the prize encouraged him to use his reputation as a vehicle for his political convictions, so too it led him to obtain greater profits from American publishers. In an unprecedented move, his agent, Carmen Balcells, sold *Chronicles of a Death Foretold* (1983) to Knopf and Ballantine with the stipulation that they have the right to publish it for only ten years. She also demanded ten-year time limits from Harper and Row for *One Hundred Years of Solitude* and other books on that publisher's backlist. Abiding by the rule that the publishing rights continue as long as the books are in print, Canfield rejected Balcells's demand. García Márquez had learned from and improved on Fuentes's techniques.

Undoubtedly, García Márquez is a canonical figure of the late twentieth century. Each new novel he publishes becomes a major literary event. Leading authors like Thomas Pynchon, Anne Tyler, or Margaret Atwood are usually invited to review his new work. In 1988, when Knopf issued *Love in the Time of Cholera*, Pynchon praised it lavishly and attributed revolutionary qualities to the text. He argued that the novel had recovered for both the "ever subversive medium of fiction" and a culture "which is paranoid about love"[98] the belief that immortal love still exists. Margaret Atwood was no less dazzled by *The General in His Labyrinth* (1990), a novel about the last months of Bolívar.

Though these two novels left Macondo aside, his *Love and Other Demons* (1995) returned to that realm of magical realism. Both the work and persona of García Márquez foster myths about the "outsize realities" of Latin American culture and life. As critic Johnny Payne stated, "García Márquez makes it very clear that . . . exotic everyday phenomena are not only exceedingly difficult for Latin Americans to articulate but are, in his estimation, by their very prolific nature almost beyond the imaginative grasp of Europeans (and by implication, of North Americans)."[99]

If Fuentes triumphed by befriending the power brokers of the New York publishing world, Julio Cortázar resorted to a more unorthodox strategy. In the mid-fifties he met Paul Blackburn, who took a shine to his mystical, experimental works—*Final del juego* (1956) and *Las armas secretas* (1959). Blackburn got a hearing for his Argentine friend at Pantheon Books, thanks to his wife Sara, also a writer and then employed as a secretary to the managing editor. In 1965 Pantheon issued

Cortázar's novel *The Winners* in a translation by Elaine Kerrigan. It was greeted with unexpected enthusiasm. William Goyen in the *New York Times Book Review* found echoes of Melville in the rhythm of Cortázar's language and seemed quite transported by his metaphysical speculations.[100] Unfortunately, Goyen's endorsement did little to advance Cortázar's American career. His poor commercial performance made it harder for Sara Blackburn to push for the publication of *Hopscotch*, his major work. In Latin America, the novel had been hailed as a masterpiece; in Europe it had been praised for the immense variety of its narrative structure. The readers contracted by Pantheon agreed with European reviewers: "I turned the pages as eagerly as though reading a first class mystery novel, simply to find out what would happen next."[101] Blackburn and the outside readers were so excited by the novel that Pantheon reluctantly took on the book in 1965. Blackburn went all out to make *Hopscotch* a success in the United States. Impressed by Rabassa's work in *The Odyssey Review*, she hired him to translate the novel. Rabassa's superb ear for the novel's wordplay and innuendoes had much to do with the effective writing relationship, and later friendship, the author and translator developed. Rabassa described their translating strategies as follows: "I would send a few chapters to Julio in Paris for his comments and he would send them back and I would send the final copy to Pantheon. It was piecemeal, but it seemed to have worked out well. At least it is an 'authorized' copy as far as the author is concerned."[102]

Blackburn combed New York for the right reviewers. Of all her choices, Donald Keene, professor of Oriental languages at Columbia University turned out to be the most discerning. He stressed the universal appeal of the book: "It is precisely because the gauchos of the pampas and the other literary baggage of South American particularism are absent from this novel that Cortázar transcends our immense ignorance of his country to move us and make us his companions."[103] Cortázar's "snapshot narration" and his "howlingly funny humor" were more important for Keene than his cosmopolitan credentials. Other reviewers dwelt on the fact that Cortázar had been living in Paris since 1961 and that Antonioni's "Blow Up" derived from his story "Las babas del diablo."

Donoso tells us that *Hopscotch* became the "object of a kind of cult in the universities."[104] A professor at Dartmouth claimed that it sold well for a period of three years.[105] Blackburn and Rabassa did not agree with such optimism. The editor recalled that the first hardback edition sold about 1,000 copies. The book, Rabassa added, despite earning good reviews and its P.E.N. translation prize, never gained wide readership.[106] Cortázar's reputation has generally remained confined to the narrower public of critics and academics. This can be explained perhaps by the hermetic nature of his fiction.

Cortázar's next American title, *End of the Game* (1967), showed him at his best—clever, funny, and not overly self-conscious. Like *Hopscotch*, however, its appeal was limited. As for *Cronopios and Famas* (1969), it fell short of his admirers' expectations and irritated reviewers in its tendency to "overmanage" flights of fancy.[107] Cortázar's mixed performance apparently prompted his publishers to seek center support for his next three books—*A Model Kit* (1972), *All Fires the Fire* (1973), and *A Manual for Manuel* (1978). While the first two provided good examples of Cortázar's bent for making fantasy intrude into familiar settings, the political implications of the last drew the most attention. *Manuel*'s disjointed narrative deals with terrorism and political kidnapping as perceived by Latin American exiles in Paris. The book's favorable reception owes much to Cortázar's visit to New York months before its publication. He was there to attend a translation conference sponsored by the center. Frank MacShane capitalized on the author's disapproval of the Argentine military regime to call attention to the currency of the novel's politics. Cortázar's incursion into politics, however, did not affect his overall American performance. Editor Wendy Wolf commented to Gregory Kolovakos at the center that [*Manuel*] puttered along as Cortázar was wont to do.[108]

Cortázar's career in the United States curiously reflects on his personal ambivalence toward U.S. culture. On the one hand, he paid lip service to the idea of Latin intellectuals' resisting the lure of capitalism: "Sigo creyendo que el intelectual latinoamericano . . . no debe ir allá, porque de alguna manera eso forma parte de la 'emigración de cerebros,' y lo que se puede hacer por América Latina en este momento yo creo que no hay que hacerlo por Estados Unidos." [I continue to believe that the Latin American intellectual should not go there [the United States] because that is part of the "brain drain," and what we can now do for Latin America we should not do for the United States.][109] On the other, he kept close tabs on the degree of success of each of his American titles and is said to have bemoaned the sluggish recognition accorded to his work. His luckiest break came in 1980 when Joyce Carol Oates reviewed *A Change of Light* in the *New York Times Book Review* and abundantly praised the book. That same year the center deemed he was finally established and no longer needed support.[110]

As with Cortázar, fame was slow in finding Vargas Llosa. He made his American debut with *The Time of the Hero* (1966), a novel depicting brutality in a Lima military school. At home the book had earned him a reputation of an "angry young man." His biographer, Luys Diez, recalled that there was "even an *auto-de-fe* when hundreds of copies of the book were burned in the parade ground of the Colegio Leoncio Prado," the setting of the novel.[111] The book's Spanish reputation led Sara Blackburn to ask Seix Barral for the option of considering it for Pantheon. Nothing came of these talks, and the book was issued by Grove Press in Lysander Kemp's translation. Its reception was minimal. His next book, *The Green House* (1968), had earned glittering reviews in Spain and Latin America. One of the readers at Harper and Row, awed by the author's "daring technique" and "skill in characterization," believed the book was bound for success.[112] American critics disagreed. Even Coleman found the book to be "considerably more extensive than compelling."[113]

Vargas Llosa's Peruvian fables grew increasingly complex in form. Canfield thought that the politics in Vargas Llosa's next book, *Conversation in the Cathedral* (1975) would discourage American readers. He suggested that a historian and not a novelist write the crucial review in the *New York Times*. Though the center could not implement Canfield's proposal, Christ was able to get the review assigned to Suzanne Jill Levine. She stressed that the novel's dizzying pattern and historical detail were not "insurmountable difficulties."[114] Michael Wood supported Levine and declared, in the *New York Review of Books*, that the challenge posed by the novel was not gratuitous, but really worthwhile.[115] To Canfield's and Christ's dismay, there proved to be few readers who took the reviewers up on their recommendations.

Captain Pantoja and the Special Service (1978) (*Pantaleón y las visitadoras*), was meant to reverse Vargas Llosa's mediocre American performance. At Canfield's request, Christ and Kolovakos themselves did the translation as well as the book's promotion. In this novel Vargas Llosa left behind the difficult, humorless nature of his earlier works and lightened up his approach. Though in Latin America this break drew sharp criticism, in the United States the book was greeted with warm reviews that commended the novel's direct narrative. The lean American version had what Christ described as its own "tale of woes" behind it. The translators were unable to impose their own and more accurate title,

Captain Pantaleón and the Ladies Auxiliary, which Christ thought "would have worked well with the double entendre."[116] Because Canfield deemed the title too exotic, they settled for *Captain Pantoja and the Special Service*. A discouraged Christ informed Luis Harss that one of Canfield's editors instituted changes without "having shown its translators either the copy-edited ms. [*sic*] or the galleys." "Canfield," he added, "has 'corrected' MVLL's grammar so that all the run-ons of dialogue and narrative are converted into discrete statements. . . . But it seems there is virtually nothing we can do unless Mario objects. Having seem him give in to the publisher on the other points, I'm not very hopeful."[117] Christ was wrong in his premature disappointment. Vargas Llosa did stand up to Canfield and demanded that his original "grammar" be respected.

Delighted by Vargas Llosa's firm stance, Christ and Kolovakos translated *The Cubs* (1979). They feared that the novel would be misunderstood in this country. Its poor commercial performance proved them right and evidently tested Canfield's patience a bit too far. Though privately an admirer of Vargas Llosa, one suspects he felt few Americans were ready to face densely allusive novels if they dealt with such remote topics as "Peruvian pathos." Regardless of Luis Harss's enthusiastic recommendation of *The War of the End of the World* (1979), Canfield turned it down and canceled his previous commitment to Vargas Llosa's fiction.

Having earlier published *Terra Nostra* and *Paradiso*, editors at Farrar, Straus and Giroux willingly made room for the Peruvian. The change turned out for the better. *Aunt Julia and the Scriptwriter* (1982) and his later, more intricate historical novels, *The Storyteller* (1989) and *Lituma in the Andes* (1993), have pleased reviewers and sold well.

Vargas Llosa's international reputation was greatly enhanced in the late 1980s when he became actively involved in Peruvian politics. During his presidential campaign of 1990, he was one of the first prominent Latin American authors, having rejected socialism, to openly advocate a free market economic model for Latin America. He lost the election and returned to literature, his first love.

Borges's and García Márquez's successes were an effective boost for younger authors like Puig, Cabrera Infante, and Sarduy. Of the three, Puig's work elicited the most critical approval. This can be partly attributed to the fact that, like García Márquez, his novels are accessible, despite their experimental narrative arrangement. Critic David Gallagher has written that Puig captures the language of his characters and reflects

their environment with "perfect naturalness."[118] Also, his subtle humor
and skillful use of popular culture—American movies of the 1940s,
journalism, and the like—conjure up easy associations for English-
speaking readers who otherwise would not be inclined to read about life
in the Argentine provinces.

With Castillo's support, Rodríguez Monegal introduced *Betrayed by
Rita Hayworth* (1971) in New York. Intrigued by the book's popularity
in Rome and Paris and its Spanish *succès de scandale*, Macrae at Dutton
signed up Puig in 1970. To the author's dismay, however, the novel
traveled a rocky road. Disagreements with Dutton over translation fees
forced Puig to cancel an initial agreement with Di Giovanni, who had
worked on the first chapter while in Buenos Aires. Puig reluctantly settled for Levine, who gave him a strong English version. He thought it
would only be necessary to give it a final revision to tighten it all up
and trim what is superfluous, a process that would undoubtedly benefit
Rita.[119]

When the novel came out it hit with remarkable force. Coleman in
the *New York Times Book Review* praised Puig for his courage to be
his own man in a country haunted by Borges.[120] In an insightful
Commonweal review, Christ was equally impressed. Despite the critical
acclaim, editor Marian Skedgell informed Puig that a third printing was
unlikely due to a drop in sales. Puig was greatly disheartened and threatened to cancel his contract with Dutton. Fortunately, the storm blew
over. The sales were better than expected and a third printing was issued.

The publication of *Heartbreak Tango* (1973) was no smoother. There
were the usual delays and misunderstandings between author and editor.
Also, whether rightly or not, Puig sensed a tepidness in his publisher,
which drove him to continually rehearse for a patient Castillo the success he had had in Europe. He reminded him in a letter that in Italy *Boquitas* [*Boquitas pintadas* (1970) was the Spanish title for *Heartbreak
Tango*] was fourth among the foreign best sellers of 1971, after Segal,
Histoire of 0, and *Charity Girl* and ahead of Gould, Uris, Camus, Irwin
Shaw, and Pearl Buck.[121] Elsewhere, he bragged about his triumph in
the Hispanic world by indicating that *Boquitas* was leading in Buenos
Aires and was for sale as well in Spain.[122] In New York the book fared
well but did not match its European record. Though it bowled over reviewers, who said it excelled *Rita* in its humor and manipulation of
popular culture, it did not make the *New York Times* best seller list. It
lingered for a few months in the *Times*'s "New and Recommended" list.

Two years later when the center subsidized the translation of Puig's *The Buenos Aires Affair* (1976) Christ's and Skedgell's hunch that the book had good prospects of breaking out of the Latin American ghetto proved to be right.[123] By the time Knopf issued *The Kiss of the Spider Woman* in 1979, it was evident that Puig had gained a devoted, if not very large, following. The conjunction of Puig's presence in New York (he was living in Greenwich Village), the plot (the relationship between a homosexual and a political activist in an Argentine jail), and Christ's adroit editing of Thomas Colchie's translation made the novel a favorite in gay circles. Christ ran a long interview with Puig for the gay journal *Christopher Street* and turned him into a household word in gay communities across the country.[124]

In the mid-1980s *The Kiss of the Spider Woman* gained a wider readership when it became the basis for the movie of the same name, for which William Hurt won an Oscar as best actor. It was also turned into an award-winning Broadway hit produced by Harold Prince.

Puig's *Eternal Curse on the Reader of These Pages* (1981), was the ultimate proof of his sophistication about things American, including language. The novel is set in Greenwich Village and written directly in English. Though it did not match the appeal of *Spider Woman*, *Tropical Night Falling* (1991), his last novel, ensured his status as the most distinguished author of the post-boom period.

Cabrera Infante's fiction draws on everything Puig's does: American pop culture, humor, nostalgia (for pre-revolutionary Havana night life) in a language that is close to speech. Yet his career has not attained comparable heights. Cabrera's *Three Trapped Tigers* (1964) won a string of European awards and aroused Castillo's and Christ's hopes for a similar New York performance. They did all they could for the novel. The center subsidized the translation, which was done by Levine and Donald Gardner in close collaboration with the author. *Review* ran a focus on the book and Castillo threw a reception on the eve of its publication. The book got friendly reviews. Cabrera was fortunate to have his friend David Gallagher review it for the *New York Times Book Review* and assert that the novel was one of the most genuinely experimental works ever to come out of Latin America.[125] In *Commonweal*, Christ likened Cabrera's "high jinks" and puns to those of Joyce and Sterne's.[126] Roger Sale in the *New York Review of Books* spoke glowingly of his recreation of Cuban slang.[127] The reviews sold few books (by 1979 it had only sold about 2,000 copies), and the novel's length—461 pages—and its overt "literariness" kept readers away. John

Updike may have spoken for the typical American reader when he complained of the novel's "fearful air of congestion, of unconsummation."[128] Christ was too amazed by the Cuban's genius to deprive him of a second chance. He got center support and publicity for *View of Dawn in the Tropics* (1978). But instead of making headway against reader indifference, the book deepened it. Unlike *Tigers*, critics were lukewarm. Cabrera waxed philosophical about his American showing. After all, when he thought of the silence that surrounded Borges in Buenos Aires and Nabokov in Berlin, who spent sixteen years teaching English while he wrote in Russian and published in small editions what today are considered masterpieces, he felt he should not complain.[129]

The case of Sarduy is not easily distinguishable from that of his fellow Cuban Cabrera. Sarduy's French reputation, derived from his close association with *Tel Quel* and Roland Barthes, did not carry over to New York. His disturbingly avant-garde *Cobra* (1975) found readers only in the minuscule community of followers of structuralist criticism or those who enjoy verbal juggling. Comparing Sarduy to Thomas Pynchon, an impressed reviewer commended Levine's translation and confirmed the book's elusive texture: "Of course *Cobra* isn't for everybody. . . . For those who desire fiction that is unsoiled, that has reasonable insights, a pleasant story, and identifiable characters, stay away from *Cobra*."[130]

Beset on every side by success-minded publishers, Christ and Castillo managed to uphold the cause of other experimental and even more hermetic books. No novel illustrates the center's faith that in time ambitious, demanding works might find a general readership better than Lezama Lima's *Paradiso* (1966). Relying on Cortázar and Vargas Llosa's claims that the Cuban's "many rooted baroque" belonged in the same class with Proust and Joyce, Castillo persuaded Roger Straus to sign it up in the late sixties.[131] The labyrinthine story behind *Paradiso's* American translation in some way resembled the novel itself. The blockade against Cuba prevented getting a copy of the book, and contacting the author was an even more difficult problem. When it was first published in Havana, *Paradiso* had been somewhat of a *succès de scandale* because of its explicit descriptions of homosexual love. Its aestheticism and Castro's disapproval of homosexuality and nonpolitical literature quickly relegated the novel to oblivion and the novelist to public disfavor. After long negotiations with Alejo Carpentier, then head of Cuba's national press, and probably thanks to the good words put in by Lezama's friend Julio Cortázar, the novel got to New York.

Cortázar had helped Lezama rewrite sections of the novel and in 1968 he published the revised edition in Mexico. For the English version Roger Straus selected Elizabeth Bishop to write the prologue and Gregory Rabassa to do the translation. Lezama approved these editorial choices and wrote from Havana: "Me agrada que sea la poetisa Elizabeth Bishop la que prologue la obra. Ella ha demostrado interés por las cosas cubanas, pues hace años, en la revista *Orígenes*, que yo dirigía se publicaron unas páginas suyas sobre un poeta primitivo cubano, Gregorio Valdés." [I am glad poet Elizabeth Bishop will write the prologue. She has shown an interest in things Cuban, and years ago in the magazine *Orígenes*, which I edited, her piece on Cuban primitive poet Gregorio Valdés was published.][132] Though his eyes glowed with pleasure when offered the translation, Rabassa was well aware that the book posed one of the toughest challenges of his career.[133] Getting through to the author was almost as sinuous an endeavor as translating the novel. Rabassa's version of the first section was forwarded to Lezama by Susan Sontag, who in 1970 spent a month in Cuba and brought back his comments to New York. Later, Julio Cortázar acted as a go–between. Rabassa mailed samples of his translation to the Argentine in Paris. Cortázar would then pass them on to Cubans returning to Havana, where Lezama would scrape about to find ways of reversing the route. When the Padilla case broke, contacts were interrupted and the last segments of the translation were never revised by the author. Along with practical hurdles, the text posed exceptional linguistic and structural challenges, which Rabassa described as follows:

Lezama is trying to break Spanish out of this kind of narrow possibility as far as grammar is concerned. My previous experience with some of the new Latin American writers, like Vargas Llosa, was different. He experimented in style and in the structure of the novel, but Vargas Llosa is never messy with the basic structure of the language; that is everything he does is very legitimate. On the contrary, Lezama seems to be always trying to twist it out. . . . Lezama, I think, is making an attempt, either conscious or not, to open the language for syntactical freedom, I guess you'd call it.[134]

The translation was not ready until 1973. Whether the author considered Rabassa's rendering faithful to the impenetrable original is not known. But the fact is that even Rabassa's translation was not considered to be clear enough; editor Andrée Conrad, with the help of exiled Cuban poet Manuel Cortázar, pruned and extensively edited the final version, which appeared in 1974.

Considering American critics' distaste for the overwhelmingly baroque, Lezama fared rather well with reviewers. Though a few complained that the English version impoverished its sense of language, most acknowledged that they were in the presence of a masterpiece. Author Edmund White, for instance, spoke of *Paradiso* in these terms: "The proof of the greatness of *Paradiso* is that for the last two weeks I've been walking around New York seeing things through Lezama's eyes. . . . Lezama's language is reckless, voluptuous, sly and unrelentingly sexual."[135]

Possibly the center's next most heroic feat was its championing of Ernesto Sábato's *On Heroes and Tombs* (1981). Twenty years passed between the Argentine publication and its appearance in the United States. The book's ordeal with American publishers had Kafkaesque overtones. The story began in 1969 when Holt, Rinehart and Winston, excited by the publicity surrounding Borges and Fuentes, signed a contract with Sábato and obtained center support for a translation. Almost five years later, owing to some unexplained disagreement, Holt unilaterally canceled the contract. Sábato attributed this cancellation to Patricia Emigh's inadequate translation and not to his work. The novel had met with outstanding reviews in Buenos Aires, where it appeared in 1962, and in Europe. Bewildered and offended, he complained to Christ: "Jamás en mi historia de treinta años de literatura recibí una carta tan grosera, tan arrogante y despiadada. Es terrible tener que admitir una injusticia semejante agachando la cabeza." [Never in my thirty years of literature have I received such a rude, arrogant, and merciless letter. It is awful to have to accept such an injustice and to swallow your pride.][136]

Because of the center's opportune intervention, at Christ's behest, the novel finally found its way into publication. Outraged by the fashion in which Sábato, whose prestige in Latin America ranked with Borges and Cortázar, was being treated, the center hired a lawyer to buy back the rights to the book from Holt. The center paid Holt back the $1,100 advance Holt had given the author. Later Helen Lane, translator of Paz and many other authors, and recipient of major translation awards, was employed to produce a second English version. Despite Lane's brilliant rendering, no publisher wanted the book. Knopf, who in 1951 had issued Sábato's *The Outsider*, Grove, Viking, Penguin, and other important publishers turned it down. Its epic range and intricate style probably explain the publishers' resistance. The struggle ended when Christ arranged an agreement between the center and Boston publisher David R. Godine. After Christ's "fancy scrambling" overcame Godine's worries about financial losses, a contract was signed in 1978.[137] The center covered the full cost of the translation and is said to have allocated most of that year's Literature Program budget to this one book.

By the time these problems were settled, Sábato seems to have been in a deep depression over the whole affair. As his wife, Matilde, confessed to Rosario Santos, director of the Literature Program after Christ's resignation: "Cuando por fin podrá ver su obra . . . en lengua inglesa . . . parece haber perdido todo interés y le da lo mismo lo que suceda. En el fondo de esto hay una enorme amargura, lo sé." [When at last he will be able to see his book appear in English, he seems to have lost all interest and does not care what happens. I know that behind all this there is great bitterness.][138] Elsewhere, she referred to his fears of a weak reception, which would harm his European reputation. He had won the Medici Prize for *Abaddon el exterminador* (1974).

Sábato's apprehension was unfounded. Both the center and Godine did well by author. Robert Coover in the *New York Times Book Review* called *On Heroes and Tombs* a masterpiece. Other publications throughout the country followed Coover's lead and celebrated Sábato's talent. Only for Helen Lane was the outcome less gratifying, for most reviewers either omitted any mention of the translation or said only a word or two about it, though Lane had shown great skill in transforming Sábato's dense prose into limpid English. Christ bewailed the oversight in a letter he wrote to the *Times* in July 1981. He suggested that proper recognition of translating skills should be a matter of editorial policy and sparked a debate that brought Latin American writers to the fore. Without the input of translators and reviewers—the marginals in the world of letters, as Lane put it—the new Latin American writing would have remained confined to Spanish-speaking readers.[139]

VII

The boom in Latin American fiction stimulated American interest in other Latin writing that was formerly neglected or the province of specialists: poetry, drama, women's writing, and young novelists. Undoubtedly poetry has benefited the most. A case in point is Pablo Neruda. Though in the mid-fifties and early sixties Robert Bly, William Merwin, and their followers paid a great deal of attention to his work, as we noted in chapter 3, it was only in the aftermath of the Borges–García Márquez euphoria that Neruda became the object of intense critical interest. Neruda was accustomed to seeing his work appear in publications by small, avant-garde presses like Grove, so Farrar, Straus's acquisition of exclusive world English-language rights to his new work in 1972 was unprecedented.

Octavio Paz was something of an anomaly. He had lived in this country and was well respected by American poets. By 1968 he was an established figure. In addition to his work in journals, New Directions, Grove, and Indiana Press had published his poems and essays with far more success than Neruda enjoyed. When University of Texas Press became interested in Paz in the late sixties, Lysander Kemp lobbied for his writing with unusual vigor: "Although he writes in Spanish, [his book] is not limited to Spain and Latin America: he speaks of Homer and Shakespeare and Racine and Novalis as comfortably as he speaks of Góngora and Darío," he wrote of *The Bow and the Lyre* (1973), Paz's *ars poetica*.[140] Yet when in the early seventies the center supported his work—*Configurations* (1971), *The Perpetual Present* (1973), and *Eagle or Sun* (1976)—even Paz profited from the boom. Of all Latin American poets, he alone was mentioned in the same breath with Borges and the "nueva novela" writers.

A negative corollary of the boom in Latin American letters was that a number of minor figures and second-rate authors took advantage of the vogue and got work translated into English and published here. A sense of perspective was hard to maintain. From utter oblivion, Latin American writers moved to the center of U.S. intellectual attention. Promising writers began to be ranked in the same league with Borges or Cortázar. As some of the boom writers became commercially viable, the center shifted its emphasis to lesser-known names. More and more, in its efforts to gain a hearing for these newcomers, some of them marginal talents, it resorted to extraliterary appeals. If the writer came from Central America much ado was made of political turmoil there; if from Chile or Argentina, the issue of human rights was the password for rapid recognition. Women writers were easy: they were associated with feminism. Argentine Luisa Valenzuela's astounding rise to fame in the early 1980s is said to owe much to the backing of both the center and prominent women writers like Susan Sontag and Erica Jong. Sontag invited Valenzuela to join the Board of Directors of the New York University Humanities Council and plugged her books. Even the current interest in Chicano and Puerto Rican writers stems in part from the success of Borges and the boom.

VIII

In the early eighties the scope of the center's Literature Program changed. With the exception of the support provided for University of Texas at Austin professor Naomi Lindstrom's translation of Argentine Roberto Arlt's *The Seven Madmen* (1929), which David R. Godine published in 1984, translation was de-emphasized. Priority was given to projects like the Writers in Residence Program set up by former director Rosario Santos. A diligent organizer, Santos invited younger authors like Cuban Reinaldo Arenas, poet Enrique Lihn, and Luisa Valenzuela to be guests of the center and acquaint themselves with the New York literary community. Though the program was successful, Santos's plans suffered a major setback with the temporary termination of *Review*. When the Council of the Americas, a business group also founded by David Rockefeller, and the center merged to form the Americas Society, the center was replaced by the society's Literature Program, currently headed by Daniel Shapiro. It continues to promote Latin American literature and art through its journal *Review*, cultural activities, and occasional publicity support for newer authors. Since 1985 the society has sponsored only three translations, including Nicanor Parra's *Antipoems: New and Selected* (1985).

The center changed the history of Latin American literature in this country. Thanks to its translating of works by almost seventy authors, a half a dozen of which have become household names among American intellectuals, more and more publishers feel comfortable with Latin American writing, and important publications no longer regard Spanish American or Brazilian works as curiosities. No other national literature has had the advantage of such creative and tireless support.

NOTES

1. For discussions of the technical innovations of the boom novelists, see D. P. Gallagher, *Modern Latin American Literature* (London: Oxford University Press, 1973), Carlos Fuentes, *La nueva novela hispanoamericana* (Mexico City: Joaquín Mortiz, 1969), and Zunilda Gertel, *La novela hispanoamericana contemporánea* (Buenos Aires: Columba, 1971).

2. José Donoso, *The Boom in Spanish American Literature: A Personal History*, trans. Gregory Kolovakos (New York: Columbia University Press, 1977), 10–11.

3. Mario Vargas Llosa, "Primitives and Creators," *Times Literary Supplement*, 14 November 1968, 1287,

4. Carlos Fuentes, *La nueva novela hispanoamericana*, 14.

5. Ibid., 36.

6. See Emir Rodríguez Monegal, *El boom de la novela latinoamericana* (Caracas: Editorial Tiempo Nuevo, 1972).

7. Donoso, *The Boom*, 19–35.

8. Manuel Pedro González, "La novela hispanoamericana en el contexto de la internacional," *Coloquio sobre la novela hispanoamericana*, ed. Ivan Schulman (Tezontla, Mexico, 1967), 67.

9. Fernando Alegría, "The Most Significant Decade in Latin American Fiction," *Publishers Weekly*, 17 September 1971, 166–68.

10. José Blanco Amor, *El final del boom y otros temas* (Buenos Aires: Ediciones Cervantes, 1976), 17.

11. Angel Rama, "Carta de Angel Rama a *Zona Franca*," *Zona Franca* 16 (December 1972), 15.

12. Sarah Crichton, "El Boom de la Novela Latinoamericana," *Publishers Weekly*, 24 December 1982, 27.

13. Raymond L. Williams, "Truth Claims, Postmodernism, and the Latin American Novel," *Profession* 92 (New York: Modern Language Association, 1992), 7.

14. See Angel Rama et al., *Más allá del boom: Literatura y mercado* (Mexico City: Marcha Editores, 1981).

15. Donoso, *The Boom*, 49.

16. Ibid., 16–19.

17. Quoted in Enrique Lafourcade, "El Crac del Boom," *El Mercurio*, 14 November 1976, 1.

18. Donoso, *The Boom*, 99.

19. See *Revista Casa de las Américas* 1 (June–July 1960).

20. See *Revista Casa de las Américas* 30 (29 January 1965), 63–80.

21. Julio Cortázar, "Carta," *Revista Casa de las Américas* 45 (1967), 9.

22. Guillermo Cabrera Infante, "What Happened in Cuba," *London Review of Books*, 4 June 1981, 4.

23. Alan Riding, "Revolution and the Intellectual in Latin America," *New York Times Magazine*, 13 March 1983, 28–33.

24. See Rodríguez Monegal, *El Boom*, 29–30.

25. Ibid., 22–24.

26. Ronald Christ to Carmen Balcells, 23 July 1975. Literature Program Files, Center for Inter-American Relations. Unless otherwise cited, all correspondence in this chapter is from the Center for Inter-American Relations.

27. See Molloy, *La Diffusion*.

28. Emir Rodríguez Monegal, interview held in New Haven, Conn., May 1982.

29. Carlos Fuentes, "Situación del Escritor en América Latina," *Mundo Nuevo* 1 (July 1966), 6.

30. See Christopher Lasch, "The Cultural Cold War," *Nation*, 11 September 1967, 198–212 and *Nation*, 26 June 1967, 802, 821.

31. Emir Rodríguez Monegal, "La CIA y los Intelectuales," *Mundo Nuevo* 13 (July 1967), 19–20.

32. In an interview held in May 1982, Mr. Rodríguez Monegal explained that after the *Mundo Nuevo* scandal broke out, he proposed to the Ford Foundation a financial arrangement that would involve reorganizing the affairs of the magazine. He also suggested the establishment of an editorial board, made up of Carlos Fuentes, Octavio Paz, and other Latin American intellectuals, to administer the financial resources of the magazine. Ford Foundation turned down the proposal.

33. For a Cuban view of the *Mundo Nuevo* affair, see Ambrosio Fornet, "New World en Español," *Revista Casa de las Américas* 40 (1967), 106–115.

34. Robert Wool to IAFA Board of Directors, 9 November 1966. Knopf Collection, HRHRC, UT, Austin.

35. Donoso, *The Boom*, 92–93.

36. Ibid., 96.

37. Emir Rodríguez Monegal, "Diálogo en Puerto Azul," *Mundo Nuevo* 20 (February 1968), 93–95.

38. See "Discord in the Cultural World," Washington *Evening Star*, 12 August 1965.

39. An analysis of the Rockefellers' interest in Latin America may be found in Meyer Kutz, *Rockefeller Power* (New York: Simon and Schuster, 1974) and Claude C. Erb, "Nelson Rockefeller and United States–Latin American Relations, 1940–1945" (unpublished Ph.D. dissertation, Clark University, 1982).

40. José Guillermo Castillo to Norman Thomas Di Giovanni, 30 July 1970.

41. Ronald Christ, interview held in New York, May 1982.

42. Guillermo Cabrera Infante to Ronald Christ, 20 June 1972.

43. José Donoso to Ronald Christ, 21 February 1977.

44. Alfred Knopf to H. Reid Bird, 1 October 1970. Knopf Collection. HRHRC, UT, Austin.

45. Alastair Reid to Edgar, 29 January 1968.

46. Ibid.

47. Norman Thomas Di Giovanni to José Guillermo Castillo, 8 October 1969.

48. Simon Michael Bessie to Margaret Shedd, 17 October 1955, Harper and Row Collection, HRHRC, UT, Austin.

49. Columbia University Press to Rosario Santos, April 1981.

50. Anatole Broyard, "The Exile Who Lost His Tongue," *New York Times Book Review*, 26 June 1977, 14.

51. Jorge Luis Borges, "The Argentine Writer and his Tradition," *Labyrinths* (New York: New Directions, 1962), 184.

52. James Laughlin to Irene Rostagno, 2 April 1982.

53. Molloy, *La Diffusion*, 194–247.

54. James Irby to Barbara Spielman, 7 September 1964, University of Texas Press Publishing Files. Authorization from Ms. Spielman.

55. Gregory Blackstock to Miguel Enguídamos, 21 May 1964, University of Texas Press Publishing Files. Permission to quote from Ms. Spielman.

56. Paul de Man, "A Modern Master," *New York Times Book Review*, 19 November 1964, 8.

57. Ibid.

58. John Updike, "The Author as Librarian," *New Yorker,* 30 October 1965, 223.

59. Ibid., 234.

60. John Ashbery, "A Game with Shifting Mirrors," *New York Times Book Review,* 16 April 1967, 4.

61. John Barth, "The Literature of Exhaustion," in *Surfiction,* ed. Raymond Federman (Chicago: Swallow Press, 1981), 23.

62. Morris Dickstein, "City Life," *New York Times Book Review*, 26 April 1970, 1.

63. Ronald Christ, "Jorge Luis Borges," *Paris Review* 40 (winter 1967).

64. Norman Thomas Di Giovanni to José Guillermo Castillo, 10 August 1969.

65. William Gass, "Imaginary Borges," *New York Review of Books,* 20 November 1969, 9.

66. Geoffrey Hartman, *"The Aleph and Other Stories 1933–1969,"* *New York Times Book Review*, 13 December 1970, 5.

67. Alfred Kazin, "Meeting Borges," *New York Times Book Review*, 2 May 1971, 4.

68. V. S. Naipaul, "Comprehending Borges," *New York Review of Books*, 19 October 1972.

69. Tony Tanner, *City of Words: American Fiction 1950–1970* (New York: Harper and Row, 1971), 42.

70. Norman Thomas Di Giovanni to José Guillermo Castillo, 10 August 1969.

71. Keith Botsford, "My Friend Fuentes," *Commentary*, February 1965, 66.

72. Donald Demarest to Simon Bessie, 7 August 1958, Harper and Row Collection, HRHRC, UT, Austin.

73. Lee Baxandall, "An Interview with Carlos Fuentes," *Studies on the Left* 3 (1962), 55.

74. *New Yorker*, 8 August 1964, 88–89.

75. Blanche Knopf to John Brown, 16 June 1964, Knopf Collection, HRHRC, UT, Austin.

76. Alexander Coleman, "A Life Retold," *New York Times Book Review*, 28 November 1965, 42.

77. Donoso, *The Boom*, 57.

78. "*Cambio de Piel* en Italia," *Mundo Nuevo* 21 (May 1968), 20–21.

79. David Gallagher, "Stifled Tiger," *New York Times Book Review*, 4 February 1968, 41.

80. Carlos Fuentes to Carl Brandt, 23 February 1969.

81. See Wendy B. Faris, *Carlos Fuentes* (New York: Frederick Vagar, 1983).

82. Ronald Christ to Carlos Fuentes, 12 June 1975.

83. See Herbert Mitgang, "On the 7th Day, the Envoy Writes," *New York Times*, 28 October 1976, 59.

84. Robert Coover, "*Terra Nostra*," *New York Times Book Review*, 7 November 1976, 3.

85. Luis Harss and Barbara Dohman, *Into the Mainstream* (New York: Harper and Row, 1966), 316.

86. Mario Vargas Llosa, "From Aracataca to Macondo," *Review* 3 (1970), 129.

87. Gabriela Canfield, interview held in New York, May 1982.

88. William Kennedy, "The Yellow Trolley Car in Barcelona and Other Visions," *Atlantic*, January 1973, 57.

89. Cass Canfield to José Guillermo Castillo, 15 July 1969.

90. Ronald Christ, "*One Hundred Years of Solitude*," *Commonweal*, 6 March 1970.

91. John Leonard, "*One Hundred Years of Solitude*," *New York Times*, 3 March 1970, 9.

92. Jack Richardson, "Master Builder," *New York Review of Books*, 26 March 1970, 3.

93. Paul West, "A Green Thought in a Green Shade," *Book World*, 22 February 1970, 5.

94. Quoted in Joseph Epstein, "How Good is Gabriel García Márquez?" *Commentary*, May 1983, 60.

95. "Hawkes and Barth Talk about Fiction," *New York Times*, 1 April 1979, 31.

96. Gregory Rabassa to Ronald Christ, 10 July 1976.

97. Marlise Simons, "A Talk with Gabriel García Márquez," *New York Times Book Review*, 5 December 1982, 7, 61.

98. Thomas Pynchon, "The Heart's Eternal Vow," *New York Times Book Review*, 10 April 1988, 1.

99. Johnny Payne, *Conquest of the New Word: Experimental Fiction and Translation in the Americas* (Austin: University of Texas Press, 1993), 27.

100. William Goyen, "Destination Unknown," *New York Times Book Review*, 21 March 1965, 5.

101. Sara Blackburn to Toni Lowry, 27 April 1965, Knopf Collection, HRHRC, UT, Austin.

102. Gregory Rabassa to Herbert Weinstock, 5 February 1966, Knopf Collection, HRHRC, UT, Austin.

103. Donald Keene, "Moving Snapshots," *New York Times Book Review*, 10 April 1966, 1.

104. Donoso, *The Boom*, 60.

105. Sarah Castro-Klarén, "Translations, Editions, Sales, Stars: A Not So Booming Boom?" (paper presented at the workshop, "The Rise of the New Latin American Narrative, 1950–75," organized by the Latin American Program of the Woodrow Wilson International Center for Scholars, Washington, D.C., 18–20 October 1979).

106. Sara Blackburn and Gregory Rabassa, interviews held in New York, May 1982.

107. C. D. B. Bryan, "Cronopios and Famas," *New York Times Book Review*, 15 June 1969.

108. Wendy Wolf to Gregory Kolovakos, 1978.

109. Ana María Hernández, "Conversación con Julio Cortázar," *Nueva Narrativa Hispanoamericana* 3 (January 1973), 40.

110. Rosario Santos to Nancy Nichols, 4 March 1980.

111. Luys A. Diez, "A Very Special Service," *Nation*, 1 April 1978, 377.

112. J. Frakes to Cass Canfield Jr., 12 December 1968.

113. Alexander Coleman, "The Green House," *New York Times Book Review*, 12 January 1969, 4.

114. Suzanne Jill Levine, "Conversation in the Cathedral," *New York Times Book Review*, 23 March 1975, 1.

115. Michael Wood, "Masquerades," *New York Review of Books*, 20 March 1975, 27–28.

116. Ronald Christ to Irene Rostagno, 16 April 1984.

117. Ronald Christ to Luis Harss, 2 September 1977.

118. D. P. Gallagher, *Modern Latin American Literature* (London: Oxford University Press, 1973), 188.

119. Manuel Puig to José Guillermo Castillo, 2 May 1970.

120. Alexander Coleman, "Betrayed by Rita Hayworth," *New York Times Book Review*, 26 September 1971, 3.

121. Manuel Puig to José Guillermo Castillo, 28 February 1972.

122. Manuel Puig to José Guillermo Castillo, 1 March 1970.

123. Marian Skedgell to Ronald Christ, 25 September (exact year not available).

124. Ronald Christ, "Interview with Manuel Puig," *Christopher Street*, April 1979.

125. D. P. Gallagher, *"Three Trapped Tigers," New York Times Book Review,* 17 October 1971, 5.

126. Ronald Christ, *"Three Trapped Tigers," Commonweal*, 12 November 1971, 161.

127. Roger Sale, "Keeping up with the News," *New York Review of Books,* 16 December 1971, 23–27.

128. John Updike, "Books: Infante Terrible," *New Yorker*, 29 January 1972, 91.

129. Guillermo Cabrera Infante to José Guillermo Castillo, 20 June 1972.

130. Jerome Charyn, *"Cobra," New York Times Book Review,* 9 March 1975, 18.

131. Julio Cortázar, "An Approach to Lezama Lima," *Review* 11 (fall 1974), 28.

132. José Lezama Lima to Roger Straus, 22 April 1969.

133. André Conrad to Lezama Lima, 3 June 1969.

134. Gregory Rabassa, Typescript, Literature Program Files, Center for Inter-American Relations.

135. Edmund White, "Four Ways to Read a Masterpiece," *New York Times Book Review,* 21 April 1974, 27–28.

136. Ernesto Sábato to Ronald Christ, 21 July 1976.

137. Ronald Christ to Helen Lane, 30 December 1977.

138. Matilde de Sábato to Rosario Santos, 30 October 1980.

139. Helen Lane to Ronald Christ, 14 August 1975.

140. Lysander Kemp, "Screening Report: *The Bow and the Lyre,*" 12 August 1968, University of Texas Press Publishing Files.

Conclusion

Today no other group of foreign authors enjoys a larger readership in the United States than Latin Americans. By examining the efforts waged by Americans to make Latin American writers known to U.S. readers, this book has traced the history of hemispheric cultural and po litical relations, American literary tastes, and the strategies of U.S. publishers.

Until 1960 the tide of literary influence between the Americas flowed mainly in one direction. In the early sixties, however, the course of hemispheric literary relationships was redefined with the American discovery of the writings of Jorge Luis Borges, who became the first major Latin American influence on the work of important U.S. writers like John Barth, Robert Coover, Donald Barthelme, Thomas Pynchon, and John Hawkes. In the late seventies and early eighties, Latin American authors began to have an impact on younger U.S. postmodernist writers, who have acknowledged their indebtedness to the work of Gabriel García Márquez. More recently, women experimenting with epistolary fiction, like Fanny Howe and Lydia Davis, have shown a marked affinity with Manuel Puig's use of the genre for social commentary.[1]

Although the euphoria that greeted magical realism in the early seventies has somewhat dissipated, it is still the perspective from which most Americans view Latin American writing. In the 1940s and 1950s most reviewers and publishers dismissed Latin American literature as exotic; now it is loved for its fantastic, mythical, and tropical power. With the exception of Puig, the most successful postboom authors have been women, who, like Isabel Allende and Laura Esquivel, continue to deftly mingle magic and politics and to perpetuate the idea that there is no other sort of writing coming out of Latin America. These authors have created an export image of Latin America, which has tended to overshadow the variety of other fiction now being published in the region.

Following in García Márquez's footsteps, Isabel Allende was the first Latin American woman writer to attract a vast international audience. She made her U.S. and European reputation with the best-selling *The House of Spirits* (1982). In addition to enchanting readers with artful storytelling, it reinforced the notion that in Latin America magical realism is not just a literary device but makes up the fabric of everyday life. When interviewed, Allende insists that even in her own life the line between fantasy and reality seems to blur. She delights journalists and campus audiences with tales about her clairvoyant grandmother, who could move a sugar bowl "across the table with her mere gaze," and memories of her great aunt, "who at the end of her life began to sprout the wings of a saint."[2]

Though less skillfully structured, her subsequent books, *Of Love and Shadows* (1987) and *Eva Luna* (1988), also relied on exotica, sex, and politics and sold quite well. *Paula* (1995), a chronicle of her life and her daughter's death, has caused some reviewers to assert that her truth is even more astonishing than her fiction. Regarded as the continent's foremost female writer, Allende has achieved a cult status as much for the magical excesses of her fiction as for her politics and family name. As critic D. P. Gallagher has observed, her popularity is partly based on a formula that has proven to be quite profitable:

Isabel Allende se dirige a una masa que quiere sentirse culta leyendo novelas latinoamericanas, porque están de moda. Su arte es de confirmar prejuicios. Dispersa "realismo mágico" a la García Márquez [y] en lo político ubica a los buenos y malos con relajante simplismo. Agrega un toque—¿por qué no?—de feminismo para destacar el detestable machismo latino y refuerza su chic político con el cuento de que es la sobrina exiliada de Salvador Allende.

[Isabel Allende appeals to a public that wants to feel sophisticated by reading Latin American novels because they are in fashion. Her art is that she confirms prejudices. She sprinkles "magical realism" à la García Márquez [and] in politics very casually separates the heroes from the villains. She adds a touch—why not?—of feminism in order to highlight the detestable Latin machismo and reinforces her political chic with the story that she is the exiled niece of Salvador Allende.][3]

Isabel Allende's fame opened doors for the Mexican screenwriter Laura Esquivel, who has cooked up her own variety of magical realism. In 1992 Doubleday published *Like Water for Chocolate*, a novel that blends magic, romance, family history, and elaborate food in surprising ways. Helped by the film version, the book was on the *New York Times* best seller list for over seventy weeks. Encouraged by this success, Doubleday bought the Spanish-language rights for the United States and Canada and published the novel for Hispanic readers.

In the last fifteen years the boom celebrities have continued to publish work that is important and widely acclaimed. Along with Isabel Allende, these authors have tended to monopolize public attention and to obscure a significant body of Latin American work by a variety of younger, lesser known authors, who explore different universal issues and are not meant to be read primarily for what they tell us about the region.

Though a few university and independent presses, like Frank Janney's Ediciones del Norte, have consistently exposed U.S. readers to new voices from the region, most postboom novelists have found it difficult to break into the mainstream. Due to the recession in commercial publishing in the 1980s, publishers understandably stuck with writers with proven reputations rather than experimenting with unknowns.

However, in 1995 and 1996 this situation began to change. Attracted by the growing importance of the domestic Hispanic market, large publishers renewed their enthusiasm for Latin American writing by bringing out for the first time editions in Spanish, as well as in translation. Ballantine actually translated Cristina García's *Dreaming in Cuban* (1992) into Spanish, publishing it as *Soñar en Cubano* under its One World imprint. Harper Libros issued simultaneously English and Spanish editions of Isabel Allende's *Paula*. Vintage Español signed an agreement with Alfaguara, a Spanish imprint belonging to Santillana. The publisher plans to issue more than thirty-six titles to be distributed in the United States and Canada, including José Donoso's *Donde van a morir los elefantes* (1995). In addition, they will publish works by Mexicans Angeles Mastretta, Eugenio Aguirre, and Juan Villoro and Chileans Gonzalo Contreras, Jaime Collyer, and Marcela Serrano. Large houses also made room for U.S. Hispanic women, like Sandra Cisneros, Julia Alvarez, and Ana Castillo, who in the mid-1990s captured wider readership after having been confined to small, Chicano or feminist presses.[4]

Of the many reasons for recognition of Latin American writing, certainly the most important is the high quality of the fiction and poetry itself. Nevertheless, without taking anything from the achievement of Latin American literature, we must observe that Latin Americans have benefited from the U.S. missionary impulse, idealism, guilt, and self-interest. More recently, multiculturalism, in its effort to expand the canon and include so-called non-Western texts in the curriculum, has given significant impetus to Hispanic Americans, especially those with African blood, and feminists, who deal with gender, race, or class issues. They are chosen to show students the diversity of American society.

Latin American literature has been given special treatment in the American marketplace, like no other national literature has enjoyed. Devotion to this cause has inspired the promotional efforts of such odd bedfellows as a thirties critic with prophetic inclinations, several cosmopolitan publishers, avant-garde and radical editors, and a non-profit organization with strong ties to the political and corporate establishment. However different and contradictory may have been the motives, literary tastes, and successes of these promoters, the fact remains that the fortunes of Latin American literature in the United States are part of the larger history of Latin American political and commercial relations. From Waldo Frank to the Rockefellers, the support, promotion, and ultimate inclusion of Latin American poets and novelists in the canon of literature in translation have been bound up with political beliefs and ideological values.

As it often happens in literary history, numerous authors who merited translation or greater attention, like Silvina Ocampo and Alfredo Bryce Echenique, have been unfortunately overlooked. This may have occurred because either their works were not considered to be marketable or they lacked the proper contacts.

Waldo Frank shared many of the utopian assumptions of prominent intellectuals during the 1930s. In his rejection of capitalist America and in his search for an organic community, he invested Latin America with mythical qualities. Latin American culture, particularly its regionalistic literature, became a metaphor for a more natural, innocent, and humane social order and an alternative to fragmented, industrialized America.

The editors of *The Plumed Horn* partook of the zeal for social and individual transformation that had inspired Frank. Like him, they looked to Latin America in a time of crisis and endowed artists and intellectuals with a kind of moral superiority. In Margaret Randall and Sergio Mondragón's eyes, politicians had failed; only U.S. and Latin American poets could bring about a vital inter-American exchange. The editors of the 1960s differed from Frank in their preference for experimentation and in their view of Latin American literature not as an extension of "nature" or the folk, but as a part of the worldwide avant-garde. *The Plumed Horn* brought together those Americans and Latin Americans who, like their mentors, the Beat poets, abhorred rhetoric and poetic convention and repudiated mainstream social values. As the sixties progressed, Randall became more involved in the cause of the Cuban Revolution and decided that the magazine had to abandon its original pluralistic stance because she was persuaded that the diffusion of Latin American poetry in the United States, and American literature south of the border, was less important than the triumph of socialism.

The Knopfs' and the Rockefellers' commitment to the cause of Latin American literature had a significantly different motive. Linked to the political establishment and supporters of liberal democracy, they sought to make the work of Latin American authors part of mainstream American culture. Whereas the Knopfs' primary concern was with making Latin American novelists marketable, the Rockefellers wished to counteract the leftist sympathies of most Latin American intellectuals and the impact of Cuba. Part of the trouble with inter-American cultural relations, they believed, was that Latin Americans had never fully enjoyed the opportunities the American cultural scene offered. This explained, they thought, a great part of these intellectuals' resentment of the United States and their fascination with Castro's regime. The Rockefeller-funded Center for Inter-American Relations supported high-quality writing, regardless of its author's political stance. Although the center did not necessarily change Latin American writers' ideological values, nor eradicate the anti-Americanism that has traditionally dominated Latin American intellectual circles, it did make clear the U.S. respect for cultural diversity and the many benefits offered by a market economy practicing freedom of expression. However bound to the goals of American foreign policy the center's first intentions may have been, its efforts yielded surprising results. Latin American authors have come to know American culture more closely, and in many cases they have learned to draw distinctions between official policies and the opinions current in U.S. intellectual circles. Simplistic condemnations of the United States and knee-jerk fear of imperialism have often been replaced by a desire to participate and profit from what the American cultural scene has to offer. Even a rabid anti-American like García Márquez relishes his U.S. popularity and acknowledges that contemporary American culture is perhaps the most vital in the world.

Just as Latin Americans have begun to move beyond the Manichean Ariel versus Caliban interpretation of hemispheric cultural differences, American writers and intellectuals have started to overcome their stereotypes of Latin Americans. Mutual influences and richer images of the United States in the Latin American mind, and of Latin Americans among North Americans, may result in a new course for inter-American cultural relations through a dialogue independent of political vagaries. This trend will most likely be reinforced by growing economic interdependence within the hemisphere.

NOTES

1. See Johnny Payne, *Conquest of the New Word: Experimental Fiction and Translation in the Americas* (Austin: University of Texas Press, 1993).

2. Margaret Hornblower, "Grief and Rebirth," *Time*, 17 July 1995, 61.

3. D. P. Gallagher, *Improvisaciones* (Santiago: Centro de Estudios Públicos, 1992), 158.

4. Juana Ponce de León, "Brave Nuevo Mundo: Chronicle of a Merger Foretold," *Voice Literary Supplement*, November 1994, 9–10.

Selected Bibliography

Abrahams, Edward. *The Lyrical Left*. Charlottesville: The University Press of Virginia, 1986.

Anderson Imbert, Enrique. *Spanish American Literature*. Translated by John V. Falconieri. Detroit: Wayne State University Press, 1963.

Barth, John. "The Literature of Exhaustion." In *Surfiction*, edited by Raymond Federman. Chicago: Swallow Press, 1981.

———. "The Literature of Replenishment." *Atlantic*, January 1980, 65–71.

Berman, Ronald. *America in the Sixties: An Intellectual History*. New York: Harper and Row, 1970.

Bernstein, Harry. *Making an Inter-American Mind*. Gainesville: University of Florida Press, 1961.

Blanco Amor, José. *El final del Boom y otros temas*. Buenos Aires: Ediciones Cervantes, 1971.

Bly, Robert. *Neruda and Vallejo*. Boston: Beacon Press, 1971.

Brushwood, John S. *The Spanish American Novel: A Twentieth Century Survey*. Austin: University of Texas Press, 1975.

Castro-Klarén, Sarah, and Hector Campos. "Traducciones, tirajes, ventas y estrellas: El 'boom.'" *Ideologies and Literature* 4, no. 17 (September–October 1983), 319–38.

Chapman, Arnold. *The Spanish American Reception of United States Fiction, 1920–1940*. Berkeley: University of California Press, 1966.

———. "Waldo Frank in Spanish America: Between Journeys, 1924–1929." *Hispania* 47 (September 1964), 513–17.

Christ, Ronald. *The Narrow Act: Borges' Art of Allusion*. New York: New York University Press, 1969.

Conn, Peter. *The Divided Mind: Ideology and Imagination in America, 1898–1917*. Cambridge: Cambridge University Press, 1981.

Crane, Hart. *The Letters of Hart Crane, 1916–1932*. Edited by Brian Weber. New York: Hermitage House, 1952.

Crichton, Sarah. "El boom de la novela latinoamericana." *Publishers Weekly*, 24 December 1982, 26–30.

Daniel, Elizabeth. "Spanish American Travelers in the United States before 1900: A Study in Inter-American Literary Relations." Ph.D. diss., Univiversity of North Carolina, 1959.

Dickstein, Morris. *Gates of Eden*. New York: Basic Books, 1977.

Donoso, José. *The Boom in Spanish American Literature: A Personal History*. Translated by Gregory Kolovakos. New York: Columbia University Press, 1977.

El Corno Emplumado, 1961–1969.

Ellison, Fred P. *Brazil's New Novel: Four Northeastern Masters*. Berkeley: University of California Press, 1954.

Espinosa, José Manuel. *Inter-American Beginnings of U.S. Cultural Diplomacy, 1938–1943*. Washington, D.C.: Department of State, 1976.

Felstiner, John. *Translating Neruda: The Way to Machu Picchu*. Stanford: Stanford University Press, 1980.

Fernández Retamar, Roberto. *Caliban and Other Essays*. Translated by Edward Baker. Minneapolis: University of Minnesota Press, 1989.

Fitz, Earl E. *Rediscovering the New World: Inter-American Literature in a Comparative Context*. Iowa City: University of Iowa Press, 1991.

Franco, Jean. *Introduction to Spanish-American Literature*. Cambridge: Cambridge University Press, 1969.

——. *The Modern Culture of Latin America: Society and the Artist*, rev. ed. Hammondsworth, Eng.: Penguin, 1970.

Frank, Waldo. *América Hispana*. New York: Garden City, 1931.

——. *Memoirs of Waldo Frank*. Edited by Alan Trachtenberg. Amherst: University of Massachusetts Press, 1973.

——. *Our America*. New York: Boni and Liveright, 1919.

——. *Primer mensaje a la America Hispana*. Madrid: Revista de Occidente, 1930.

——. *South American Journey*. New York: Duell, Sloane, Pearce, 1943.

——. *Virgin Spain*. New York: Boni and Liveright, 1926.

Fuentes, Carlos. *La nueva novela hispanoamericana*. Mexico City: Joaquín Mortiz, 1969.

——. "Situación del escritor en América Latina." *Mundo Nuevo* 1 (July 1966), 6.

Gallagher, D. P. *Modern Latin American Literature*. London: Oxford University Press, 1973.

García Márquez, Gabriel. "Latin America's Impossible Reality." *Harper's*, January 1985, 13–16.

Gertel, Zunilda. *La novela hispanoamericana contemporánea*. Buenos Aires: Columba, 1971.

Gunn, D. W. *American and British Writers in Mexico.* Austin: University of Texas Press, 1973.

Harss, Luis, and Barbara Dohmann. *Into the Mainstream: Conversations with Latin American Writers.* New York: Harper and Row, 1967.

Hassan, Ihab. *Radical Innocence: The Contemporary American Novel.* Princeton, N.J.: Princeton University Press, 1961.

Josephson, Matthew. *Life Among the Surrealists.* New York: Holt, Rinehart, and Winston, 1962.

Kloucek, Jerome. "Waldo Frank: The Ground of His Mind and Art." Ph.D. diss., Northwestern University, 1958.

Kutz, Myer. *Rockefeller Power.* New York: Simon and Schuster, 1974.

Leal, Luis. "A Spanish American Perspective of Anglo-American Literature." *Revista Canadiense de Estudios Hispánicos* 1 (fall 1980), 61–73.

Lindstrom, Naomi. *Twentieth-Century Spanish American Fiction.* Austin: University of Texas Press, 1994.

Mead, Robert. "After the Boom: The Fate of Latin American Literature in English Translation." *Americas* 30, no. 4 (April 1978), 2–8.

Menton, Seymour. *Prose Fiction of the Cuban Revolution.* Austin. University of Texas Press, 1975.

Molloy, Sylvia. *La Diffusion de la Littérature Hispano–Americaine en France au XXè Siècle.* Paris: Presses Universitaires de France, 1972.

Mundo Nuevo, 1966–1971.

Oliphant, Dave. *On a High Horse.* Fort Worth, Tex.: Prickly Pear Press, 1983.

Payne, Johnny. *Conquest of the New Word: Experimental Fiction and Translation in the Americas.* Austin: University of Texas Press, 1993.

Ponce de León, Juana. "Brave Nuevo Mundo: Chronicle of a Merger Foretold." *Voice Literary Supplement*, November 1994, 9–10.

Rama, Angel. *La novela en América Latina.* Veracruz: Fundación Angel Rama, 1986.

———. *Más allá del Boom: Literatura y mercado.* Mexico City: Marcha Editores, 1981.

Randall, Margaret. "El Corno Emplumado, 1961–1969: Some Notes in Retrospect, 1975." *TriQuarterly* 43 (fall 1978), 405–22.

Reid, Alastair. "The Latin American Lottery." *New Yorker*, 26 January 1981, 106–11.

Review, 1970–1982.

Rodríguez Monegal, Emir. *El boom de la novela hispanoamericana.* Caracas: Editorial Tiempo Nuevo, 1972.

———. "La CIA y los intelectuales." *Mundo Nuevo* 13 (July 1967), 19–20.

———. "Diálogo en Puerto Azul." *Mundo Nuevo* 20 (February 1968), 93–95.

Stabb, Martin S. "Waldo Frank: A Very Unusual Yanqui." *Review* 47 (fall
    1993), 87–88.
Tanner, Tony. *City of Words: American Fiction, 1950–1970.* New York:
    Harper and Row, 1971.
Updike, John. "The Author as Librarian." *New Yorker*, 30 October 1965,
    223–35.
Williams, Raymond L. "Truth Claims, Postmodernism and the Latin Ameri-
    can Novel." *Profession* 92 (1992), 6–9.

Index

About the Author

IRENE ROSTAGNO is Associate Professor of English and American Studies at Universidad Metropolitana, Santiago, Chile. She received her Ph.D. in American Civilization from the University of Texas at Austin. She has published several critical articles, as well as book contributions and translations.

ISBN 0-313-29869-6

9 780313 298691

HARDCOVER BAR CODE